Garden Ma

A to Z of
Garden
Maintenance

Lynton V. Johnson

BRIZA

Published by
BRIZA PUBLICATIONS

CK 90/11690/23

PO Box 56569
Arcadia 0007
Pretoria
South Africa

First edition, first impression 2005

ISBN 1 875093 50 8

Managing editor: Frits van Oudtshoorn, Reneé Ferreira
Copy-editor: Frances Perryer
Cover design: Sally Whines, The Departure Lounge
Typesetting: Alicia Artnzen, The Purple Turtle
Reproduction: Unifoto, Cape Town
Printed and bound by Tien Wah Press (Pte.) Ltd, Singapore

I dedicate this book to the thousands of gardeners
who simply wish to enjoy gardening that much more,
and – despite all the odds –
get the gardening thing right every now and then.

And to my very dear friends Denise, Johann and Alta,
such good friends,
always there when a listening ear is needed.

"I know a bank whereon
the wild Thyme blows."
A Midsummer Night's Dream
ACT 2 SC I
William Shakespeare

CONTENTS

INTRODUCTION

Welcome to the mystical and oft-frustrating world of garden maintenance!

To begin: what is gardening? A dictionary description might say something like: 'It is the art of making and *caring* for a garden; also the work involved.'

South Africa has several climatic areas – and climate constitutes one of the major factors influencing gardening in any particular area. Therefore our gardening definition must take into account the weather ... when it rains, and how much, together with annual temperatures and any other climatic impact typical of any area.

Add to this soil types, factors such as pH, sandy or clay soils, depth or amount of soil in which to garden, position in sun or shade, and it becomes obvious that an individual definition would be needed for each and every garden. Suffice it to say that ANY garden needs to be cared for – and I hope that this book will help to make it all much easier.

Many of the topics are included because questions have cropped up again and again over the years, others because they are where the most mishaps occur and by offering early advice these may be avoided ... well, there is a slight chance, and one can but hope. Needless to say, to cover all aspects of garden maintenance in depth in a single publication would be difficult. Because of this, some of the more major maintenance topics will be dealt with in greater detail than the others. I have tried to cover South Africa's many varied regions and their garden challenges, so the user may have to refer to more than one entry in order to get the best of the information.

It is important to note that despite the constant reference to 'working' in the garden, the idea is that it should also be enjoyable and that the challenges should be undertaken in the right frame of mind. If it becomes a constant bind to maintain a garden, something is not quite right!

For many home gardeners there is a lot more of the *caring*, and little of the *successful making* of a garden. The reason for this is quite simple: much of what needs to be known about caring for a garden is learnt by trial and error, hit and miss, or sheer luck. It can safely be said that very little can be read on this vast topic. In many cases the only literature available is from the northern hemisphere, which does not realistically relate easily to the varied gardens of South Africa.

I would like to believe that with this book tucked under your arm, or at least near at hand, you will begin to feel more comfortable with the maintenance practices – basic, yet successful – typical of any domestic garden in South Africa.

In any garden, large or small, simple or detailed, a moment of maintenance leads to months of of satisfied garden splendour!

A

AGAPANTHUS

An indigenous rhizome plant, mainly in shades of blue and white; mostly evergreen, though in some areas affected by severe frost, and a few naturally deciduous species. Most varieties will tolerate some shade, but not too dark, as they tend to flower less. For more information refer to PERENNIALS and BULBS.

A touch of formality, with dwarf white Agapanthus, Agapanthus africanus spp.

ALGAE
(INCLUDING LICHENS AND MOSSES)

Where there is paving (particularly clay brick) and moisture, there will be moss or algae, or both. In some cases it's seen as romantic and encouraged because of the appearance of age it gives to clay, concrete or cement pots, statues and water features. However in many other situations gardeners are far more interested in getting rid of it. Depending on where in the garden these plants develop, there is generally little cause for concern, unless they tend to make walkways or steps slippery and unsafe. In some cases the concern should be where the moisture is coming from! A leaking pipe or tap, perhaps ...

Algae is a dark green, black or brown, slippery growth associated with water and very wet or damp areas. (Seaweeds are forms of algae.)

Lichen is a combined plant form consisting of both fungus and algae, commonly found growing as rounded, frilly-edged rosettes on rocks and tree trunks. It can be very bright green, yellow, orange or silvery grey-green.

Moss is the furry green growth found growing in such places as shaded riverbanks, paving and south-facing brick walls that are permanently damp. Often seen growing in conjunction with ferns.

Moss-encrusted paving – friend or foe!

A lichen encrusted branch – harmless even if oft unsightly.

Hint: *Spraying or painting an item with sour milk, yoghurt or 'karringmelk' encourages the growth of algae, which provides an 'ageing' effect.*

- Moss on paving or pots can be scrubbed off with a stiff brush.
- For more effective removal, dust with dry swimming pool chlorine then scrub.

- Coarse salt can be scattered to discourage algae or moss on paving. Don't apply salt where it can have an adverse affect on the condition of the soil.
- Algae can be treated with a diluted wash of swimming pool algaecide mixed 1 part to 5 parts water.
- Wispy green algae that has established itself in fishponds can be 'caught' and disposed of if tied bundles of wheat straw are floated in the water. The algae attaches itself to the straw and can then be removed and discarded. (These prepared bundles are available at pond supply shops and some koi fish suppliers.)
- UV lights can be added to some forms of koi pond filtration systems to help reduce algae in ponds. Consult any reliable koi fish or general pond accessory supplier for more information.
- Lichen on rocks and trees is quite harmless, and is generally an indication that the area is shaded or moist. Removal is not necessary.

ANNUALS

These flowering, short-lived plants are generally grown for the specific purpose of highlighting and providing colour to specific areas of the garden. Some gardeners depend almost entirely on annuals to provide colour (think of public garden plantings).

Annuals can be defined as plants that germinate, grow, flower, develop seed and die, all during the space of one growing season. It is common knowledge that there are summer and winter annuals, but it is not generally known why plants grow better during one season or another.

SUMMER ANNUALS are able to tolerate high temperatures, regular rainfall, long daylight hours and increased soil temperatures; they are usually sensitive to frost or extreme cold. Because of the length of our summer conditions some annuals will not live through the entire season, but if the growing conditions remain ideal, further plantings may take place. Extreme summer conditions may result in unfavourable growing conditions – for example, too much rain or extreme heat for long periods – in which case the plants may become diseased or die prematurely. Should summer annuals become severely infected by fungal infestations, pull them out, treat the soil with a systemic fungicide and plant new, although different, annuals. Summer annuals are often more prone to insect infestations than the winter selection, as insects are generally more active in the favourable summer conditions.

Well-known summer annuals include:

Begonia

The fibrous-rooted varieties are available in shades of red, white and

Fibrous-rooted Begonia, *ideal in semi-shade areas, is perennial in mild climates.*

pink, with bronze or green foliage, and grow from 15 cm to 30 cm. These are true shade lovers, grown from seedlings or cuttings and flowering for months on end, often only dying off when they are destroyed by frost or severe cold. New varieties that are quite tolerant to sun have been developed, extending their use in the garden.

> *Hint: Begonias and impatiens are perennial in mild climates and will readily live through winter in a protected area. Cut back after winter and boost with a liquid foliar feeder.*

Impatiens
Popular in various shades of red, pink, salmon, lilac and white, with new colours almost every year. They can grow from 15 cm to 50 cm. Although some new strains of *Impatiens* are reasonably sun tolerant, they are best known as a semi-shade loving annual.

Impatiens, *sure colour winners in light sun or semi-shade areas.*

Marigold
Available in shades of yellow, orange and bronze and growing to various heights from 15 cm to 70 cm. Recently, a cream variety has been developed. They are true sun lovers, easily grown, and can be planted out as young plants or grown in situ from seed broadcast over larger areas.

Petunia
Available in a wide range of varieties, colours and growth habits; all of them are drought and heat tolerant plants for sunny positions. They tend to behave poorly if the season or area is too wet. It is said that they grow best when the rains are over and the temperatures are still quite high – late summer and early spring. In areas where the winters are mild and dry they could be planted to flower through the winter months. There are 'perennial' varieties that can live for longer periods than the conventional annual varieties, some even making ideal groundcovers in the right conditions. As these forms of petunia have quite specific growing requirements and will

Petunias – *ideal sun-loving annuals for dry areas and seasons – don't like too much water.*

be part of the garden for longer than the annual varieties, it is important that the ideal conditions are provided before planting.

Vinca
A relatively new annual, although the tall perennial forms have been seen growing in hot, dry places all over the country for years. The newer, compact varieties (20–30 cm) are available in shades of rose, salmon, pink, and white, some with a darker 'eye' and others not. Totally at home in hot, dry positions, they make a welcome addition to the summer annual range.

Many other summer annuals, such as zinnias, phlox, portulaca, salvia, and celosia, help to make up the long list of summer annuals ideal for typical growing conditions.

Vinca *is the perfect summer annual for dry, hot areas and pots too.*

Easy to grow marigolds provide quick and easy colour for large and small sunny areas.

The very reliable pansy, perfect in every way – colour, appearance and almost any situation.

WINTER ANNUALS require quite different growing conditions. Tolerant of low temperatures, frost, short days and low rainfall, they include great favourites such as primula, poppy, pansy and viola. Winter annuals tend to become untidy, unattractive, and prone to severe attacks of green aphid as the weather warms up in late spring. This can be seen as a gentle reminder that it is time to plant summer annuals.

Winter annuals tend to prefer sun to shade, which rather limits the options for winter planting. The vast ranges of colours and hybrids of shade-loving primula, pansy and viola amply make up for this, however. Remember that if deciduous trees cause the shade, this will be drastically reduced during the winter period, creating an opportunity to plant annuals that enjoy either partial shade or sun.

A few annuals do not have a specific growing season. *Alyssum*, *Lobelia* and petunia can be planted all year round in mild dry areas and in some cases will self-seed throughout the year.

As annuals are all grown to provide colour, it is wise to remember some pointers:

- Blue and purple are cool colours and should be used sparingly in winter.
- Bright colours such as red and orange should be used in limited quantities if the area is small.
- If there is space, use bright colours away from living areas.
- Balance very bright colours with pastel colours or white.
- Use a balance of single-colour plantings and mixed-colour plantings so as not to have an overall blotchy effect.

- Annual colour should enhance and be in harmony with other aspects of the garden rather than contrasting too severely with them – make sure you know what colour the annuals are before planting them.
- White flowers harmonise well with any plantings, permanent or otherwise.
- Pastel colours are better than bright ones for small areas such as townhouse gardens.
- Use annuals in selected areas to provide colour highlights to otherwise monotonous plantings.

The last word on annuals

- Low-growing annuals flower quicker than tall ones and are ideal for late season planting.
- Some annuals grow better from seed sown in situ – nasturtium,

sunflowers, *Zinnias*, sweet peas, Namaqualand daisies and *Cosmos*, for example.

- Removing dead heads will prolong the flowering life of an annual.
- All annuals give best results if the plants are young, healthy and not root-bound when planted.
- Annuals respond well to regular foliar feeding, particularly when they are coming into flower.
- Never plant annuals too deep, and don't over-cultivate the soil between them.
- Make sure that they are not planted too close together or too far apart.
- If birds eating the leaves are a problem, cover young seedlings with a bird net until the plants are strong and well established, or push branches in between the seedlings as this makes it difficult for the birds to land.
- Cutworm losses can be reduced by dusting the soil with cutworm bait before planting, or if there are not too many seedlings to plant, wrap each one in a newspaper collar and plant with 2 cm of the paper protruding above the soil.

ANTS

There are numerous ant species but only a few of these are of any concern to the gardener. The large **black garden ants** that are seen scurrying about on hot dry days are more annoying than destructive, but they do tend to create numerous small, dry, granulated soil heaps between paving, at the edges of flower beds, against the stems of plants and in the lawn. This is cause for annoyance because it blunts cylinder mower blades, is unsightly and makes some garden surfaces difficult to keep clean for any length of time. They do not kill plants, but their subterranean activities can undermine seedlings and other young

plants, which tend to fall over if the ant activity is excessive. Ant bait is available and is quite effective. Paraffin lightly sprayed on paving and other hard surfaces in areas of ant activity will discourage them – but make sure that the paraffin cannot be washed onto herbaceous plants or lawn, as it will kill them.

The **small black sugar ants** found in houses and outside under garden objects are in themselves relatively harmless. However some species of these ants live off the 'sundew' excreted by aphids and some scale insects, and tend these insects for this purpose. Any ant activity up and down the stems of citrus and Australian tea-bushes is a sure indication that these plants are infested with either aphids or scale, and the likelihood is that a black mould will be apparent on the stem areas too. The ants grow the mould on the harvested sundew. Control of these ants will help to eliminate the black mould, but total control will only be effective if the aphids and scale insects are treated.

The house-invading versions are easily controlled with ant traps and available baits or sprays.

Termites are not strictly ants, other than in a vague appearance way. They live off 'dead-wood', in other words trees that have died in the garden, the thick corky bark of some living trees and untreated timber products. The earthy crust that often covers such wood is a sure sign of their presence and when it is removed or washed off the pale cream and brown insects can be seen, hence the common name of 'white ants'. Because most wood used in gardens today is sealed or treated, their destruction is not as apparent as it used to be. However they can still quite easily destroy the wooden railway sleepers or slices of untreated logs popular as informal walkways in the garden. (See WOOD for solutions.) There are several baits that can be used, but

easier than that is to treat any wood used in the garden.

Harvester ants are also not a true ant, but a form of termite that cuts off grass and carries it down to colonies underground. The tell-tale bald patches with holes in them found in dry lawns during winter, in the summer rainfall areas, are a sure sign that these termites are at work. Often they can be seen, and heard, whilst active in the late afternoon or on overcast days. Because their colonies can spread over large areas, this is not a simple task for an individual gardener: when bait or poison is used, they simply move into other parts of the colony until the treatment is rendered ineffective – and then they return. Control must be a communal project, and often requires the help of fumigation experts. Impregnated dried grass baits are an effective short-term solution.

Red ants, also known as 'fire-ants' because of the painful bite they can give any unsuspecting person sitting on the grass relaxing after a picnic, are in fact harmless, and tend to drift through gardens foraging after small insects, some other ants and scraps of discarded foodstuffs. They do not have nests to speak of, and seldom stay long in any one area. Despite the pain they can cause, they are strictly beneficial insects, and should rather be left alone than eradicated.

APHIDS

Small pear-shaped insects, with or without wings, green, grey or black in colour – sometimes known as greenfly because the green aphids are so common in gardens. Aphids occur in colonies that attack flower buds and soft, new growth of plants, deforming or killing them. They are found on both indoor and outdoor plants. There are birds and beneficial insects, such as ladybirds and praying

A gardener's worst enemy, aphids love any soft new growth and are active almost all year round.

mantis, that live off them. Environmental control of aphids is simple; wash them off plants with a strong jet of water; plant garlic or false garlic lily (*Tulbaghia* species) amongst roses or other areas favoured by them; spray with strong-smelling organic sprays to ward them off. (See ENVIRONMENTAL CONTROLS.) There are a number of chemical sprays, some of them especially formulated for aphids; these are perhaps a better idea than a wide-spectrum general insecticide.

 AQUATIC PLANTS
These could simply be regarded as plants that grow in, under or on water. Upon investigation, however, several more interesting aspects of aquatic plants will be apparent.

Aquatic plants grow at various depths under water. Some only need their roots covered with a few centimetres of water, such as water irises and papyrus varieties. These usually grow on the edges of rivers, streams or ponds. Others grow below the water and their

leaves rest on the surface, while the flowers appear above them. Such is the case with water lilies and *Aponogeton* (waterblommetjies). Yet others drift in or on the water quite unattached to any soil, and lastly, there are those that grow entirely below the water, with foliage, flowers (insignificant) and seeds all forming below water level. This is typical of many of the common fish tank plants.

- Aquatic plants should not be confused with plants that look good growing *near* water, many of which will not grow well if their roots are too wet.

- Generally aquatic plants are quick growing and dormant during the winter months. They need to be divided during the early spring months before the new growth matures too much.

Aquatic plants, nature's own water purifiers; their foliage contrasts add extra appeal to any water feature.

Water lilies, exotic or indigenous, add great summer colour to water features, but are winter dormant. (Some can die in extreme cold.)

- Feeding these plants is difficult, particularly if there are fish in the same pond. A liquid organic foliar feeder could be used if practical to do so. This would be sprayed on the leaves. (Generally in a well-balanced pond the plants will be fed naturally by way of decaying vegetation and fish waste.)

- As many of them tend to float if not planted in a container, it is wise to use either clay pots or plastic baskets to grow plants in (nothing that will rust or fall apart under water). A plastic laundry basket cut down to size is ideal for this, as it won't rust or become brittle under water. Some commercial baskets are available, but their sizes are limited.

- An ideal growing medium is 50% kraal manure and 50% peat moss mixed together. As this mixture also tends to float, once the plants have been planted, cover the surface with a layer of fine stone or coarse sand.

> *Hint: When planting water plants, use a piece of plastic shade cloth to hold the growing medium and tie it loosely together at the 'neck' of the plant. A heavy stone or half brick can be placed at the base of the 'bag' to give it added weight.*

- Aquatic plants need to be controlled from time to time so that they do not congest the water area. Split them up and replant every two or three years,

in spring, before the appearance of the new growth. First remove all dead material from the plants and use this as part of the growing medium or add it to the compost heap.

- Most aquatic plants tend to frost off, but this is simply a natural part of their life cycle. After they have been frosted they can be cut back at any time before the appearance of new growth.

- It is not essential to have a pond or stream to grow aquatic plants. A large, interesting waterproofed container filled with the correct amount of growing medium and topped up with water will readily serve as a home for a miniature water lily, water iris, or similar interesting aquatic plant.

BEDDING

The long-practised art of planting out beds of annuals is known as bedding – which is why annuals are sometimes referred to as 'bedding plants'. This style of gardening was once popular in parks and around important public places such as the Union Buildings, as well as on middle islands along major urban roadways. Cost is always a factor, however: today many of the bedding areas in public places have been grassed over or planted with permanent plants to reduce the seasonal expense of annuals and their upkeep.

Generally the designs used were formal, or at least geometric in appearance, often including well-grown specimens of a striking foliage plant or flowering shrub as a focal or repeat element within the design. These were costly displays, with uniformity of plant size and growth essential to the final effect. More often than not, single-coloured annuals were used, combined with low hedges or a formal edging to the planting. Less popular today, these designs tend to be reduced in size and format, and smaller versions are often

seen as focal points at the entrance to public buildings and residential or office park complexes.

Now that formal gardens are becoming popular once again, there is often a call for

For the best effect when setting out annuals, make sure they are evenly spaced apart.

a simple bedding design, within the larger overall design. These beds are seldom informal, but the same requirements would apply if the design were to take on a softer, more informal appearance.

Points to consider

- Annuals chosen should not vary too much in height unless the taller plants can be planted at the 'back' of the design against a wall or solid shrubbery. Alternatively, the taller varieties could form the focal or central point to a planting that is viewed from all sides.

- The plants should be planted close enough together to completely cover the area as they develop.

- Choose plants that will all begin flowering at the same time.

- Replace dead or unhealthy plants before the other plants are too advanced. It might be a good idea to grow a few in pots for a few weeks, to 'add-in' where necessary.

- Keep the designs simple but accurate; use string to set out rows, and avoid curves unless there is a means of ensuring that they all look the same. Previously, templates were cut to control these aspects of the designs.

- Keep the plants healthy and feed often.

- As focal points, consider the use of plants such as standard *Fuchsias*, *Azaleas*, roses, *Hibiscus*, or conifers. Tidy specimen plants, such as *Hydrangeas* in bloom, *Pelargoniums*, palms or ferns, can also be left growing in their containers. They are removed and replaced with something else when no longer effective or dramatic enough.

- These bedding displays are entirely seasonal, and generally the whole display would be removed at the end of the season and a new design implemented for the next season. Naturally the low hedge or edging would be retained in this case.

Applications today could include the centre of traffic circles within office park or cluster complexes; raised planters or window boxes; along narrow areas such as against walls or driveways, and as focal points in paved areas or on patios.

BOG GARDENS
This type of garden makes a suitable home for many aquatic plants, and can be linked to a more conventional fishpond or stream. It is an attractive yet simple means of coping with a spring, seasonal seepage or annoying damp area in the garden.

Bog gardens are simple to construct and as simple to maintain. Seldom is there any noticeable water, so mosquitoes cannot breed. They are simply areas where the growing medium stays constantly moist, such as the banks of a typical river or earth dam.

Construction is simple. Excavate the intended area to a depth of 30–50 cm. Line this with layers of plastic, which needs to be perforated all over with small holes 50–75 cm apart to allow the water to rise up through the plastic or seep away. A non-waterproofed, 6–7,5 cm thick cement or clay layer would serve as well. Perhaps even more simple is to mix a bag of cement with the top 10 cm of the soil once the shape has been decided and excavated, moisten and stamp into shape. One bag of cement should cover 10 square metres. Mix the excavated soil with kraal manure and peat moss, one third of each, refill the 'hardened' shape, water well and begin planting.

Select plants that grow well in these conditions and will create interest all year round. Consider some foliage material to balance the

A well-balanced bog garden edging a man-made stream.

The giant leaves of Gunnera manicata *perfectly contrast with the finer foliage of many bog plants.*

flowering material. If some plants tend to be invasive, plant these in their own 'net baskets' or a plastic bucket with a few holes made in the bottom.

If the area is viewed from all sides, plant the taller specimens in the centre and decrease height towards the edges. If there is a specific viewpoint, place the taller plants towards the 'back' of the area and the smaller, flatter ones nearest the 'front'. To add a 'third dimension', a few select taller plants can be planted among the low plants nearer the 'front'.

Most plants found growing in vlei areas or on riverbanks will grow in bog gardens. They can be propagated either from seed or by removing a small clump of the plant (do this only where permission is obtained).

A few plants worthy of mention

Gunnera manicata – giant round rough leaves, growing into a rounded form 1,5 metres tall and wide. Very dramatic if space allows.

Gunnera perpensa – an indigenous relation of the above, with much smaller foliage and growth habit, but still dramatic as the 10 cm round leaves act as an ideal contrast with the strap-like leaves of many bog-garden plants.

Lobelia cardinalis – 80 cm tall, with deep maroon foliage and vibrant red flowers: a striking plant throughout summer.

Schizostylis coccinea (now called *Hesperantha coccinea*) – an indigenous rhizome with red, pink or salmon flowers in summer.

Phygelus capensis – Cape fuchsia, an indigenous small shrub with clusters of brick red or lime green flowers. Relatively tender, but provides an ideal contrast and background to the upright grass-like plant forms.

Marsilea quadrifolia – water clover (in reality an aquatic fern): a 'four-leafed-clover'-like plant, which grows almost at ground level. Readily found in local vlei areas. It grows well from plant division and a small clump will soon cover a reasonably large area as a groundcover.

Iris species – grown in containers in ponds and bog gardens, where their sword-like leaves add interest during the year, highlighted by various coloured flowers in spring. Most are reasonably hardy and easy to grow. They would need to be split up every three to four years.

Regrettably, many of the European plant varieties are either not available or do not grow well in this part of the world. Make sure when selecting plants from books that they are available locally.

Because of seeds in the local peat moss used in the growing medium, some vlei grasses or sedges will germinate during the growing season. These make interesting uninvited additions to the plant selection, *but* along with these there is the chance that bulrushes will also germinate. This is a very invasive plant and should be removed or restricted to a limited area.

Although some bog-garden plants are evergreen and not affected by the winter, other are deciduous and die back after the first frosts. Many of these, particularly the grasses and grass-like plants, have interesting winter colour and form: enjoy their off-season effects, and cut them back just before spring. Others can be tidied up once they are totally dormant.

The size of a bog garden is irrelevant, as even the smallest area will need very little maintenance other than division of the plants from time to time and fertilising during the growing period. Use organic fertilisers and a light layer of dry, sifted kraal manure in spring for the best results. A dusting with bone meal in spring, applied at the rate of 50 g per square metre, will prove to be beneficial.

BULBS
(AND OTHER UNDERGROUND MARVELS)

Most people think of spring flowers when bulbs are mentioned, but there are 'bulbs' for all seasons. The name often incorrectly covers a whole range of reproductive 'root' systems from which plants will grow. Commonly included under this title are:

- **Tubers**, from which potatoes, sweet potatoes, *Dahlias*, *Begonias* and even truffles grow.
- **Corms**, which produce indigenous spring flowers such as *Gladiolus*, *Freesia*, *Dierama*, *Sparaxis* and *Ixia*.
- **Rhizomes**, which produce *Agapanthus*, *Iris*, *Canna*, *Clivia* and runner-type grasses.
- **Liliums**, which are basically a cluster of soft plant scales with a central growing point, including the ever-popular St Joseph's lilies among many others. All *Liliums* are recognised as true bulbs.
- **True bulbs**, such as daffodil (narcissus), 'grape' and common hyacinth, *Amaryllis*, onion and garlic.

Needless to say, almost all the plants collectively known as 'bulbs' have different growing requirements and times of seasonal performance.

Winter/spring bulbs

'Bulbs' can be simply divided into three categories, the most popular being the winter/spring group. Well-known names such as *Anemone*, *Ranunculus*, daffodil, tulip, Dutch iris, hyacinth, *Freesia* and *Sparaxis* are purchased and planted each March, April and May.

These cool-season plants need the change of temperature from winter to spring to get their biological clocks

Summer gardens – a riot of colour with Dahlias *in the foreground adding their touch!*

Dahlias are an ideal long-flowering, perennial summer tuberous plant for sunny areas.

A stately stand of Gladiolus *– a hybridised indigenous corm.*

A host of golden daffodils – what better to announce spring?

Dutch Irises are spring-flowering bulbous 'throwaway' annuals.

Liliums in their many forms and colours are perfect summer perennial bulbs for both the garden and containers.

working. All of them are dormant when purchased and totally without foliage.

Their needs are simple: well-prepared soil including compost and fertiliser, regular and thorough watering (*but* not over watering – the '3 F' rule is Don't Forget to water for Forty minutes every Four days – unless the soil is heavy and poorly drained, then water according to drainage potential). Finally, they need to be planted at the correct depth and distance apart. When these simple needs are seen to, each one planted will grow and flower. Some plants such as daffodils can take up to 10 weeks to push leaves through the soil, and continual care during this period is essential.

> **Hint:** *If the soil tends to retain too much moisture and there is a chance of bulbs rotting, plant them on a small platform of coarse sand dropped into the bottom of each hole.*

> **Hint:** *If bulbs are expected to grow among other plants, mark their positions with small sticks – or plant the other plants first. Avoid damaging the bulbs when planting the other plants. This will lead to the bulbs rotting.*

Some winter/spring bulbs are regarded as annual and discarded once the flowering season is over. These are Dutch iris, *Anemone*, *Ranunculus*, tulip

and hyacinth. Others, if fed and watered until they go dormant naturally, and not damaged or waterlogged during the dormant period, will return during their next flowering period. Remember, to get maximum effect during the next season, it is essential to feed after they have finished flowering and until they become dormant. This can be done by way of pre-packed bulb fertiliser, liquid foliar feeding or balanced granular fertilisers.

Bulbs can be lifted and stored once fully dormant and replanted at the correct planting time. Store in a cool, dark place, either in open-weave plastic bags or in paper bags. If the bulbs are grown in pots to bloom indoors, once they have finished flowering they can be tipped out of the pots, soil and all, and 'laid-in' somewhere in the garden where they can be cared for until they are dormant, lifted and stored.

Summer bulbs

The second category of 'bulbs' is those usually planted to flower in summer. Many of these are evergreen, but the deciduous ones – such as *Lilium*, *Dahlia*, tuberose, *Amaryllis* and *Gladiolus* – can

A well-balanced display of many of the summer-flowering 'bulbous' plants.

Clivia, *a perennial, evergreen, shade-loving, indigenous rhizome for spring colour. They grow well in containers too.*

be purchased and planted while still dormant. Planting and caring for these plants is the same as for those planted during autumn (spring-flowering bulbs). If there are good rains during the summer, be careful not to over-water the plants, until they have produced leaves above the ground. Make sure the areas where they are planted are well drained, and if not, add sufficient clean coarse sand (pool filter sand is ideal) to the soil during initial preparation to improve the drainage. The sand should be dug into the top 30 cm of soil.

Evergreen bulbs

The third category consists of bulbs and related plants that are evergreen and can be dug up and replanted at any time of the year. However, it is not wise to transplant them before or whilst they are in flower. *Clivia* and several other indigenous bulbs don't like to be moved too often.

Propagation of these plants is by division of large established clumps into smaller clumps. The size of each clump depends on the size of the original plant. In the case of plants such as *Clivia* and some *Agapanthus*, don't over-divide the plants. Rather keep the clumps at three to four plants; this helps the plants to recover quicker. If the plants multiply rapidly, sub-division can take place every three to five years. When these plants are divided for replanting, discard the older parts and plant only the younger growth. This applies particularly to *Iris*, *Canna* and other tuberous or rhizome-type plants. If the plants are not divided from time to time their ability to flower regularly may be reduced. There is the chance that after division the plants may take a season or two to begin flowering again.

All evergreen bulbous material should be fed regularly during the growing period and watered well, yet not too often, during the non-growing period. If the plants are to flower early in the growing period, before the beginning of the rains, it is essential that they receive regular, thorough watering for at least six weeks before the flowers opening – i.e. from when the buds or flower spikes begin to appear.

CLIMBERS

Climbers have the ability to provide greenery against walls, on fences, arches, summerhouses or screen panels without taking up too much space. Perhaps the major problem with creepers is their ability to escape from the area intended and become too large to be managed without stepladders, long-handled loppers or professional assistance.

Perennial creepers are either self-climbing – which means that they will naturally attach themselves to the surfaces they grow against, or they may need assistance, by way of frames, pegs or wires.

The type chosen will determine how easy or complicated their attachment methods will be. It is wise to know in advance how big the creeper will become, as well as its growing habit. A light wooden frame will not be of much help if a robust creeper is expected to grow on or over it for any extended period. Make sure that the 'frame' is sturdy enough and requires reasonably low-key maintenance. This will relieve the necessity for excessive cutting back of the creeper when general maintenance of the support is required.

Structures such as gazebos, screen panels and fences should be constructed of materials that require little or no maintenance, yet at the same time, be constructed of material sturdy enough to support the weight of the maturing creeper. Tanalised treated wood, stone/brick work or galvanised metal would be ideal materials.

Should the creeper be a self-attaching species, such as ivy, make sure that it is planted against a surface that will not need regular maintenance – avoid plastered and painted walls. In the case of deciduous, self-adhering creepers (Boston Ivy for example), wait until winter, when they have lost their foliage, to attend to any paintwork or cutting back.

The harmony of the 'Golden Shower' Pyrostegia venusta, *massed dwarf marigolds and the 'gold' brickwork make a welcome entrance to any property.*

Easy to grow and quick to bloom – a good cover-all in limited spaces.

Pruning of creepers is a often a big job, yet too important to avoid. Keep the number of main stems limited to those closest to the surface on which they grow, preventing too much growth away from the support or the surface. This is particularly important in the case of very vigorous creepers, banksia roses, *Bougainvillea*, *Bignonias* (now listed under so many new names), Zimbabwe creeper or climbing roses, for example. Remove on a seasonal basis at least 30 per cent of the smaller branches, young growth and dead flower spikes. This will reduce weight and encourage new flowering growth.

For deciduous creepers (and roses, including banksias), prune out roughly one third of the growth, either in winter or once the flowering period is over.

Should you prune creepers in winter there is the chance that some of the flowering wood will be removed: this is often the case with early spring flowering plants such as jasmine, *Wisteria* and banksia roses. Evergreen creepers can be pruned at any time during their growing season; if they are non-flowering creepers such as ivy, they are pruned to keep them limited to a specific size and position.

It is a good idea to drastically reduce the size of vigorous creepers at least every three to four years, cleaning out dead foliage and spindly growth, and generally reducing the size of the creeper. As in the case of jasmine, this is usually done just after the flowering period, before the initial burst of new growth. The plant can be reduced to a few select stems reasonably near ground level. When the creeper provides some form of supported shade canopy, such as on a patio or summer house, retain a few stems up to the area to be covered (the pillars, walls or poles), and remove all or at least 80 per cent of the covering growth; this stimulates new growth but reduces the likelihood of dead material on the underside of the plant where the top covering growth excludes so much light that the plant cannot grow properly. This is done to provide a leafy canopy to look up at, rather than the woody, dead parts of the covering creeper.

In the case of annual or very light creepers, such as *Clematis*, a light or temporary frame can be provided during the growing season and replaced when the plants are removed or pruned.

Constant seasonal growth control is essential, particularly if there is the likelihood that the plants may begin to overgrow neighbouring plants or damage structures – gutters and roof structures, for example.

Hint: *Where frames are used to grow creepers against a wall, attach large hooks to the wall and hang the frames from these. They can be unhooked for wall maintenance as well as creeper control.*

Hint: *If creepers won't attach themselves to pre-cast concrete walling, cut 'spot-welded' metal mesh to the required size, firmly fold over the top of the wall and peg in place at the bottom before planting the creepers.*

COMPANION PLANTING

Much has been written throughout the history of gardening about how some plants grow better in the company of certain kinds of plants and perform badly when grown near others. This is known as companion or compatibility planting. It is widely practised when growing vegetables and herbs, and no harm will come from trying the concept when the next lot of vegetable seeds need to be sown. The list that follows is a simple one; there is far more comprehensive literature available.

	Companions	Antagonists
Asparagus	Tomatoes, parsley, basil	–
Beans	Most vegetables and herbs	Onions, garlic
Beetroot	Onions	Runner beans
Cabbage family	Most vegetables	Tomatoes, runner beans
Carrots	Lettuce, peas, tomatoes, onions	Dill
Chives	Carrots	Peas, beans
Cucumber	Beans, peas, radish, sunflowers	Potatoes, aromatic herbs
Eggplant	Beans	–
Lettuce	Carrots, radish, cucumber	–
Onions, garlic	Tomatoes, lettuce, beetroot	Peas, beans
Parsley	Tomatoes, asparagus	–
Peas	Most vegetables and herbs	Onions, garlic, potatoes
Radishes	Peas, lettuce, cucumber	–
Spinach	Strawberries	–
Tomatoes	Chives, onions, parsley	Cabbage family, potatoes

The best results in the 'veggie' garden come from good company – plantwise that is!

Companion planting often proves its worth when an environmental approach to gardening is being considered. Garlic planted among roses keeps aphids away as well as contributing to better growth and health of the roses. Marigolds planted in the vegetable garden discourage a wide range of insects as well as eelworm (nematodes). *Nasturtiums* improve the condition of the soil and, planted near fruit trees, discourage fruit flies. *Artemesia* sp. or rue planted in several places throughout the garden discourages animals from running in the flowerbeds. Basil improves the flavour of tomatoes, but it won't survive if planted near rue. There are many similar examples of companions – including weeds – that have helped simplify one or another aspect of gardening; as avant-garde as they may seem, they are certainly worth trying.

COMPOST
All too often, this is taken as simply a means of disposing of garden and household refuse ... but no matter how long it stays in a heap or hole, it will not become compost!

Compost making is quite simple, and space is no longer a major factor, as several 'bin'-type compost makers have been designed that are extremely effective yet need reasonably little standing space. The most effective compost-making techniques are either the bins mentioned or the more conventional heap. A pit may seem like a good idea, but this is not so! There is limited control over quality, inaccessibility makes it difficult to remove mature compost, and too many plant nutrients are leached into the surrounding soil.

The heap system can be constructed either in a contained area with removable sides for access to the heap, or simply level off an area, cover it with a hard surface, old paving blocks, brick, cast concrete or redundant pre-cast wall panels would suffice. This area need be no larger than 3 x 5 metres. Construct a heap that is no wider than can be worked properly from both sides (1,2 metres). Length is determined by the amount of material and when it is available. However, it is wiser to make smaller heaps, which can be built on a regular basis, rather than wait months to complete construction of one large heap.

What is required is a balance of equal amounts of coarse and fine organic material. If specific material is not currently available at the time of construction of the heap, stockpile what you have until there is a balanced amount of coarse and fine material. Coarse material can be things like shrub and light tree prunings and any other dead organic material – dead annuals, maize or sunflower stalks or similar rough stuff. To this can be added bones, thicker roots or branches and even flattened tins. All of these items will break down, albeit slowly, adding value to the compost. The fine material can be lawn clippings, leaves, vegetable peelings and dropped fruit during the season.

Firstly spread a 30 cm layer of coarse material, 1,2 m wide, on the hard surface. Should it not be enough to cover the entire length of the proposed heap, it can be extended later. Add to this a 50 cm layer of fine material. Mix lawn clippings with leaves and other material rather than in solid layers. Lawn clippings tend to compact as they rot and do not break down organically.

Continue alternating coarse then fine layers until the heap is roughly 1,5 metres high. If there is access to chicken litter, leaves of comfrey, marigold or foxglove, these can be scattered lightly between layers as an organic means of encouraging healthy decomposition. Should the plant material available be generally quite acid, such as pine needles or oak leaves, a dusting of agricultural lime between the layers could be applied. Use no more than 50 g per square metre.

Once the heap is the desired height and length it can be watered and covered with a sheet of black plastic or soil. If a compost activator is used it would be applied at the time of watering. If the heap is covered with plastic, regular watering will not be necessary as evaporation is limited. Soil-covered heaps would need regular watering.

Allow the heap to stand for 6 weeks, turn it over with a fork and allow to stand for a further 2 weeks, sift to remove the non-decomposed larger pieces (which are added to the next heap) and the compost is ready to use. Well-composted material should generate sufficient heat to kill off weed seeds as well as most insect eggs or larvae.

The 'bin' systems are simpler: continue to add a mixture of coarse and fine material until the bin is full. The adding of an activator is optional. Once the bin is full allow it to stand for a month, then remove from the bin, fork over and use.

Compost should be used regularly, as a mulch as well as when planting. Sifted through a fine sieve it will make an ideal seed sowing medium and seed covering for in-situ sown seed. If there is a need for acid compost, milled pine bark, pine needles or oak leaves would be liberally added to the heap or bin. Avoid using too much sawdust, if this is readily available, as it draws too much nitrogen from the surrounding material to assist in its decomposition. (This is known as denitrification – the removal of nitrogen from the soil by decomposing plants.)

Composting
Making compost is in some respects easier than applying it – properly. It is hoped that the compost used, home-made or purchased, will be filled with beneficial bacteria and nutrients ready to enhance the soil it is to be added to. It is senseless to scatter a little of it over the surface of the shrubberies or vegetable garden and expect it to make a difference to the quality of the soil, however. The chance is that a lot of time and money will be wasted. For maximum effect it is better to apply the compost (or manures) to small manageable areas one at a time.

- If a bed is to be replanted with vegetables, annuals, bulbs or perennials, spread a 20 cm layer over the area and dig it in with the final soil preparation before planting.

- If a new bed is intended for various plants, a 10 cm layer spread will suffice because there are no feeder roots in the area yet, but more compost will be added to each hole as these are prepared for shrub or tree planting.

- If the compost is being applied as a mulch among established plants, *lightly* dig over the area first, applying appropriate fertilisers, and then spread a 10–20 cm layer over the softened soil. This is usually not dug in.

- When planting new plants, make a hole at least twice as wide as the pot or plant bag and half as deep again. Remove a third of the soil from the resulting heap and replace it with an equal amount of compost (or well-rotted manure) and mix together well, adding the required fertilisers at the same time. Place this mixture into the hole and plant directly into it.

- Don't allow compost to lie indefinitely before using it, and try to prevent it from drying out, because it will lose much of its nutritional value.

CONIFERS
Conifers are a unique range of plants, origi-nating mostly in the colder parts of the northern hemisphere. (A few interesting conifers are endemic to the southern hemisphere, though.) Well known for their very tidy, specific plant forms, sizes and foliage colours, they have become popular throughout the country as focal or accent garden plants.

Because there is such a wide range available, from flat-growing groundcover forms to tall, thin, pencil-like forms, and a vast array in between, they suit gardens of all sizes. Among their greatest attributes is that they are evergreen, make very little mess, and if the right choice is made, seldom need to be pruned. All of them are tolerant of most South African climatic conditions, with limitations along the coastal strip perhaps; they grow at a reasonable rate, and many of them are shade tolerant, whilst the others thrive in full sun. None of them flower in the visible sense of the word, but some of them bear a cone of one kind or another. Generally the most popular conifers are the compact, colourful,

A well-established, well-selected conifer planting adds a special elegance to any garden space, particularly in cold areas.

smaller varieties, although there are large pines and cypresses all over the country.

Many conifers have typical, fine, dense needle-like foliage, but there are a few exceptions. The yellowwoods of South Africa, *Podocarpus latifolius*, *P. henkelii* or *P. falcatus*, don't look much like their European and American cousins; neither does the beautiful deciduous *Ginkgo biloba* from Japan, with its maidenhair fern-like leaves which turn bright yellow as they begin to drop in autumn. Another very beautiful conifer is the 'swamp cypress', *Taxodium distichum*, which turns a bright copper orange in autumn. It is deciduous, needs damp cool conditions to grow well, and is not too slow, but is a very large tree with time.

The yellow, blue-green, grey-green and deep green varieties will all grow easily in the sun, but the yellow or pale green forms do not grow well in the shade.

When selecting conifers for a garden, clarify their final sizes, as many of them look well shaped even when small and retain this shape until they are a lot larger. Their well-formed young shapes tend to mislead people into thinking that they will remain quite small or that the conifers are 'miniature', which is often not the case.

Don't plant conifers too close to one another, as they tend to die off where they grow into each other. Although they are very easy to grow, it must be remembered that they need water during prolonged dry periods and reasonably good, deep soil. These are not plants for hot, shallow soil situations.

Conifers are generally pest and disease free, and it is only in recent years that there have been any problems worth discussing:

A mottled effect comprising small areas of dead and dying branches all over the plant. The 'winter active Mediterranean aphid' travelled down through Africa from the Mediterranean. It attacks some conifers species of all ages and sizes, sucking sap from the young soft growth whilst at the same time 'injecting' toxic saliva back into

these branches. This causes the young soft growth of the tree to slowly die off. This is usually only apparent a few weeks, even months, later. Control of this is reasonably effective if started in the late summer months of March and April. Use a granular systemic insecticide scattered over the entire area the plants cover and watered in well; continue with this every 3 weeks until August.

Large dead areas or whole dead branches, concentrated mostly in the lower parts of the plant. 'Root rot' or Phytophthora is a water-borne fungus that moves through the soil by water seepage or movement of surface water. The first symptoms are usually branches near the base of the plant yellowing, browning and then dying off. Later, whole individual branches begin to die off. It can apparently be treated with systemic fungicides, but often the tree's shape is ruined: conifers seldom recover their shapes after branch losses, this results in the entire plant losing its natural form. Removal is another solution. Some varieties are less affected than others: enquire at your local plant stockist.

CONTAINERS

There are no specific do's and don'ts regarding which containers to grow plants in, but it is important to bear the requirements of the plants in mind. Root space, drainage and the type of material from which the container is made will have an effect on growth. This is of particular importance if the plant is to grow in the container for any length of time.

Try to create harmony when selecting containers, not only in relationship with one another, but with the area, structure and other accessories used in conjunction with the containers. Bear in mind such aspects as house style as well as the material from which the containers are made when making a selection, so that the end

effect is of a 'whole' rather than a jumbled oddity.

The initial planting up of containers should provide ideal growing conditions for the plants chosen. Correct growing medium and perfect drainage (not too little or not too well drained) are essential primary considerations. Remember plants do not naturally grow in containers, and that some will not do all that well in a restricted growing space. Should this be the case, time and effort would be wasted trying to encourage the stragglers. Choose plants that are known to grow well in containers, and select the plant and container for the best overall effect.

The plant may need re-potting from time to time, so make sure that the shape of the container allows for easy, non-damaging removal (the opening should not be too narrow), or buy containers that can be destroyed to remove the plant. When re-potting, make sure that the plant is not planted any deeper or shallower than in the previous container. If it was extremely root-bound, remove some of the roots with a sharp knife or pruning shears (no more than 20 per cent). Dust the severed roots with flowers of sulphur or a systemic fungicide before re-potting. It is important that the drainage holes do not become blocked: cover them with a synthetic drainage fabric or small clean gravel (not so small as to fall through the hole). In very shallow containers a simple method is to use a square cut from an old sock or stocking and placed over the hole before filling the container with soil.

Hint: To plant into painted containers without dirtying the surface, drape a collar of newspaper over the rim and leave it there until the container is planted, placed in position and watered. Simply remove the paper after this by tearing it off along the wet soil line, leaving the container clean.

Correct feeding of containerised plants is very important, because as the container is watered the water moves through the soil and out, taking the required nutrients with it. This can easily leave the plant underfed. Liquid foliar plant foods are ideal as they are readily absorbed through the foliage as well as the roots, in which case fewer nutrients wash away. If organic products are used they will not burn either roots or foliage. If the plant is expected to produce flowers or fruit, a regular (every 6 weeks) application of superphosphate is essential. Apply this at the rate of 15 g per small container, 30 g per medium container and 50 g per large container.

Pruning, splitting-up and re-potting are essential to keep most container-grown plants healthy. Do not wait until the plant is pot-bound before doing this. Replant tender plants in early summer when all fear of frost has passed; deciduous plants can be re-potted in winter and evergreen plants during their growing period, after flowering, but not too near their dormant period.

If a plant growing in a container has stood facing a specific direction for several years it is important to realign it towards that direction after it has been re-potted. To simplify this, mark a branch which faces north with a piece of cotton, nail varnish or paint, and once the plant has been re-potted, make sure that the marked branch again faces north.

> **Hint:** *To avoid the 'bald back area' common to plants standing in one position for too long, rotate the container slightly every 2–3 months.*

Containers selected for indoor plants often have a built-in drip tray or no drainage holes at all. To ensure that the plant receives enough water, insert a length of rigid plastic pipe down the inside edge of the container. Rigid electrical conduit is ideal. As the plant is watered, water will rise up in the pipe and can be gauged by inserting a

Containers add emphasis, either of colour or form (below) or classic elegance (right), whether they are seasonal or permanent.

Succulents are ideal companions to specialised or hand-crafted containers.

wooden dowel-stick into the pipe and reading the water level off the stick. (The wet area is clearly visible on the wood.) Indoor plants seldom need watering more than once a week and there should be no water in the pipe by the end of the week. If there is still water in the pipe, too much water is being given. The watering programme can be monitored in this way. Do not water more than once a week unless the pipe is dry before the end of the week, in which case slightly increase the amount of water applied weekly, checking and, if required, increasing again until the balance is correct. It may be necessary to water less in the off-season (winter) unless the area or room where the plant stands is heated, which could result in an abnormally higher level of evaporation.

CUTTINGS

When soft new growth or mature woody parts of a plant are rooted as a means of propagation these pieces of the plant are called cuttings. Two forms of cuttings are useful to the domestic gardener – soft- and hardwood cuttings.

SOFTWOOD CUTTINGS are taken from plants when the initial surge of new growth begins to mature (any time from mid-September onwards, depending on the specific area). Only the top 15 cm of growth is cut and used. The cutting is cut clean below a leaf or pair of leaves. The lower leaves are removed, the cutting is dipped in a soft-wood rooting hormone, and inserted into clean sand or a balanced mix of peat and sand. Seed trays or deeper containers can

also be used. Seal the container in a clear plastic bag after watering the cuttings, making sure that the plastic does not lie on the cuttings (use wood skewers or similar to hold up the plastic). Roots should develop within 4–6 weeks.

These cuttings can be taken at any time during the summer growing period, but later summer cuttings take a while longer to root. When rooted, carefully remove from the sand and transplant into a general growing medium until established and plant out into the desired final position. Many shrubs, herbs and perennials can be grown in this way – a great kiddies' project.

HARDWOOD CUTTINGS are sections of mature wood, usually dormant and prepared as cuttings during the winter months. When hardwood material is pruned from such plants as roses (some varieties work better than others), *Hydrangeas*, golden privet and May bushes, select a few straight branches 50 cm long (use the middle section of the branch – no growing tips). Cut the bottom of the branch clean below an 'eye' or bud, and cut the top above an 'eye' or bud. Dig a trench in a part of the garden where the cuttings will be cared for (or use a deep container like a paint tin), and fill with well-composted topsoil. Insert the trimmed branches, upright, half-way into the soil and water well. Roots will develop during the following growing season, and when the plants are again dormant they can be planted out into the garden.

DETERRING DOGS, CATS AND OTHER ANIMALS

It is often said that gardens and animals don't go together – but they can, if an effort is made to discourage animals from digging or sleeping in flowerbeds.

Mechanical methods of excluding domestic pets or undesirable wildlife can simply consist of sturdy fences, a scattering of thorny material such as rose prunings or thorn tree branches. A single wire firmly attached to knocked in metal stakes, or droppers, and strung around or through beds at a height of 30–50 cm above the ground will often suffice. More dramatic, yet harmless, are electrical systems designed to emit an electrical shock on contact with charged wires. These can be purchased in kit form, or experts can install them. Bird nets can be draped over areas destructively favoured by birds. Plastic 'scare' figures of cat faces can be hung to scare off flying intruders. Plastic 'snakes' will help deter weaver birds if slung into trees and if draped along the lawn are said to discourage dassies

and rabbits from visiting the garden.

Environmentally friendly chemical methods consist of scattering mothballs or naphthalene flakes sparingly over the areas favoured by the animals. Rags or rope soaked in creosote help keep animals from eating vegetables and seedlings. Commercially available sprays and pellets can be scattered or sprayed over specific areas and one part Citronella oil mixed with 10 parts light, plant-friendly, oil such as cooking oil has a reasonably long-term yet safe effect. Bunches of lavender placed in the roof deter rodents and bats; spray areas with 'Jeyes' fluid or creosote if swarming bees are a problem. Rue, *Artemisia* and garlic lily (*Tulbaghia*) serve as a deterrents to bees, moles and some rodents. Dusty Miller (*Cineraria*) and onions are said to deter rabbits (dassies too); so too are smeared animal fat on rocks and tree trunks, and blood or bone meal sprinkled among the plants.

A logical way of promoting harmony in the garden would include keeping the areas where animals run plant-free, or planting plants with spines or thorns, patches of weaverbird-friendly grass,

beds of catmint for the local 'moggy', and bird-feeder areas for the feathered gardeners.

Love or hate them, domestic pets will use garden spaces to dig, lie or play in, so make life easier for all concerned – create a space for them.

 EARTHWORMS

Apart from the obvious conclusion that soil that can support the needs of an earthworm must be quite good, few people consider earthworms and their role in soil enhancement. Most people complain about the small heaps of soil or castings pushed up on grass areas without too much thought as to what it is, where it comes from and what nutritional value it has. It is in fact highly nutritional waste created as the earthworms move through the soil foraging on organic material.

Some facts about earthworms

- They bring up minerals from the subsoil and deposit them in soluble form throughout the topsoil.

- It is estimated that earthworms move between 10 and 50 tons of soil per 4 000 square metres (an acre) per annum. The lower figure refers to poor, compacted soils and the higher to rich, friable garden soil or farmlands.

- Earthworms consume organic debris, liberating nutrients previously held in living plant tissue.

- In the course of burrowing, earthworms increase the availability of oxygen, water, and nutrients below the surface.

- They break down larger soil particles into smaller particles and by doing so improve the structure of the soil.

- When earthworms appear above the surface after heavy rains it is an indication that the soil is water-logged and they are escaping drowning by moving to the surface.

- In areas with sufficient organic material, such as fallen leaves in an undisturbed shrubbery, orchard or forest, earthworms are said to recycle up to 10 tons of material per 1 000 square metres per annum.

Nature's little helpers, earthworms are a sure sign of happy garden soil conditions.

- When the adult earthworms die, nitrogen stored in their body tissue is rapidly released (up to 70 per cent in two weeks). This is usually during summer, when plants are at their peak growing season. Earthworms are thus an excellent natural fertiliser, high in organically generated plant nutrients.

- In ideal soil conditions, earthworms multiply rapidly, allowing the process to continue.

How to breed earthworms for the garden

Select a level, well-drained site. Dig a 60 cm cubic hole, larger if you wish to line it with bricks or concrete blocks. Line the base with chicken wire to protect the worms from moles or other predators, such as toads and mice. Prepare a bedding material of equal parts manure, peat moss and soil, or equal parts organic material and topsoil, or 100 per cent organic material, such as damp leaves. Well-rotted horse manure will also work well. Fill one third of the hole with the bedding material and water if necessary. It must not be soggy or puddled with water. Add collected or purchased earthworms, between 10 and 50 worms, into a small hollow in the bedding material. (They will begin to burrow to escape the light.)

Add food directly above the bedding. Food can consist of kitchen scraps, garden refuse, wet leaves, rotted kraal, dog, rabbit, or horse manure, maize meal or even seaweed. Small quantities of shredded cardboard or sawdust could also be included. (They grow rapidly on animal products such as well-rotted manure, because of the high protein levels, and grain meals such as bran or maize meal.) Cut a piece of old carpet the size of the opening and lay it direct on top of the food. Keep this carpet damp. Cover the hole with a board to prevent it becoming hot and dry, and to prevent pets from digging in the organics.

Hints:

If using fresh manure or other rich wastes, check regularly to see that the bed does not overheat.

- *Only add small amounts of any material that may heat up, at any one time, or turn the material regularly. Food should take up no more than half of the remaining space.*

- *Because very watery organics, such as lettuce or fallen fruit, tend to 'sour' the bed, add sparingly and mix with other, drier, organic material.*

- *Don't add food too often; once a week should suffice, but wait for bare patches of bedding to appear before you feed again.*

This system will allow some worms to burrow and 'escape'; this is quite in order. If they are content they will remain, breed and increase.

Don't allow the bedding to become heavy and compacted – fork over lightly ('fluff-up') once every two weeks. Replace the bedding every six weeks as you harvest or divide your worm crop, and add the old bedding to general garden beds, vegetable gardens, etc. Earthworms prefer a reasonably neutral pH. If the material added is acid, breeding will slow down. In this case sprinkle a handful of agricultural lime over the bedding once a month.

In ideal conditions, worms need to be harvested every six weeks, and at most every three months. If bedding consists mostly of castings, or adult worms move to the sides, it is an indication that the bed is overstocked and it is time to harvest the adult worms.

Harvest on a cool or mild day with good natural light. With a fork, small scoop or hands remove half of the worms and bedding to a new site – pre-prepared as before. Alternatively, remove all the bedding, placing it onto a piece of plastic or board. The worms will move downwards away from the light. Brush off the bedding slowly and all the worms will be trapped against the plastic or

board. (Use bedding and castings as compost in beds.) Have a bucket of moist soil or compost handy to put the harvested worms in so that they do not suffer from heat or dryness. Keep back enough worms to continue breeding and add them to a new amount of bedding; add excess to further beds or encourage friends to start their own breeding bed.

EDGING

Basically, this can be regarded as a means of keeping one part of the garden from encroaching into another. It can simply be a worked (trimmed) edge to a shrubbery; an inlaid manufactured edge of plastic or metal, or a more sophisticated finish incorporating bricks, stones, logs, tiles or other garden building material.

The simple bed edge is perhaps the most common – and in most cases the least reliable: it changes shape as it is maintained, reaches unnatural heights, more for visual than practical effect, and can in many cases detract from the original, simple purpose. At best it should be shallow, simple in form, easy to retain and maintain, non-hazardous to people using the garden and almost insignificant in appearance. Many of the deep, wide trenches created, start out as a means of preventing kikuyu grass from growing into the beds. This would work if this grass didn't have the ability to grow 50–70 cm below soil level. Regular, shallow lawn edging will control the lawn better and obviate the need for the 'trench'.

Constant, dedicated edging of beds on the part of the gardener takes time and in some cases serves no purpose whatsoever. It is not uncommon to find a worked edge against a solid fixed edge – a lawn edge against a paving edge, for example. If the mounded soil, heaped up because of regular digging in these places, were simply raked back to a level just below the lawn level, and the exposed soil area filled with plants, control would instantly be simpler. The edge could be firmly and constantly held in place with one of several manufactured edges available. The lawn runners could be controlled at this edging without fear of the bed getting any larger.

Any fixed form of edging will dramatically reduce the regular maintenance of the area. It doesn't have to be conspicuous; some are installed at lawn level and simply separates the lawn from planted areas; another may keep pebbles, gravel or bark in place. If design calls for a specific demarcation, e.g. two contrasting groundcovers, edging can be installed to simplify control of the plants.

Edging should not only separate the plants from lawn or other plants but should look good too.

ENVIRONMENTAL CONTROLS

There is a growing tendency to look for alternative methods of controlling or preventing pests and diseases. These can be anything from home-brewed insecticides using home-grown control plants, to simple user-friendly garden practices. (Regular applications of homemade environmental controls will require regular harvesting of the control plant, and thus multiple plantings – one plant will seldom be sufficient.) In some cases manufacturers are introducing environment-friendly chemical products. These are designed to have low impact on the environment yet control the problem.

It must be remembered that environmental control in the garden may not always be as quick, or as constant a method as typical chemical controls. Many environmental controls do not kill off the bugs, but rather deter them. Some of them will need regular reapplication, as they biodegrade quickly or are rendered too weak to be effective by watering or rain.

> *Hint: An ideal aromatic deterrent spray can be made up of a whole head of garlic, a cupful of green chillies and a handful of rosemary leaves or 'khakibos' leaves (or both). Liquidise all these together and add two litres of boiling water. Allow to stand for two days, strain well, add a teaspoonful of liquid soap and use as a spray. This will need to be re-applied after rain or watering.*

Environment-friendly practices

- Plant shrubs and trees to encourage local bird and insect life into the garden.

- Plant clumps of weaver-friendly grasses (even sugar cane) to keep weaver birds from destroying the tropical palms.

- Keep soil covered with plants or mulch to prevent compaction, weeds, erosion, etc.

- Remove weeds manually while they are young and not in flower, to prevent distribution of weed seed. Do not allow pulled weeds to die in areas where germinating weed seed will create problems later on.

- Don't dig over beds more than is absolutely necessary – once or twice a season at most. Dug-over ground dries out quickly, loses some of its nutritional value and becomes an ideal place for weeds to germinate.

- To discourage weak, unhealthy growth, make sure the correct plants are used in the correct areas. Ask for information *before* buying and planting.

- Keep a notebook of environmental practices that prove to be of benefit.

- Water and feed as required – but do both properly each time.

- Make a study of products available and their applications, rather than blindly buying 'brand names'.

- Study your property from a climatic viewpoint to assess where the wet, dry, hot, cold, protected and exposed areas are. Use these areas to the plants' advantage.

- Keep tools clean, sharp and sterile, especially those used for cutting and pruning (use bleach or any household steriliser).

- Seal any cuts larger than 5 cm in diameter made in perennial plants with a suitable sealant to prevent entry of disease through the plant cells. Seal these cuts as soon after cutting as possible, allowing no more than a day or two for the cut surface to dry.

- Make sure that plant material introduced into the garden is healthy, and pest and disease free. Where possible, wash the soil off the roots of plants introduced into the garden from sources other than reputable nurseries and garden centres. Plant immediately. If plants appear to be unhealthy, cut back after planting, spray with a fungicide, or treat for insect control.

Many environmental controls appear to be rather avant-garde. However strange they seem, if they solve a specific problem they are worth practising. As this approach to gardening advances, more solutions will be introduced. Keep a record of them – often they are simple, cost-effective and based on products readily available.

FERNS

Ferns are a large family of non-flowering plants, often associated with cool, damp, shady growing conditions. Some ferns are reasonably hardy; others are a lot more sensitive to extreme growing conditions. Many ferns available from nurseries and garden centres are sold as indoor plants, and are not intended to be planted in outdoor garden situations. This does not mean, if the growing conditions are ideal, that they won't grow outdoors; it's more a question of more homes having better indoor growing conditions for ferns than homes with ideal outdoor conditions. One fact remains: for most ferns moisture, humidity and well-composted growing conditions are essential, well-lit yet shaded from direct sunlight (especially the severe west afternoon sun). If grown indoors, spray the foliage with water from time to time during the heat of the day and throughout the dry months of the year. Even stand a bowl of water nearby during winter, especially if a heater warms the room in which they are growing.

Ferns are quite greedy feeders: very few of the more freely available ones will grow in exposed, poor-soil situations. Regular feeding with any liquid fertiliser will help the continual development of new foliage as well as keeping the existing foliage in peak condition. If they are grown as container plants, don't replant too often – but don't allow then to become pot-bound either. If the fern is a variety with a multi-stem type of growth, and has become too large for the container, rather than repeatedly increasing the size of the container, split the plant carefully into two or more smaller plants. This division usually takes place when no new foliage is being produced

Dicksonia antarctica *is a gracious, hardy fern that is more sun tolerant than many other ferns.*

Semi-mature Cyathea australis *adding elegant height to a section of a garden.*

– at the tail end of winter or after the initial burst of new growth.

Ferns do not have flowers and do not make seed in the conventional sense of the word. Mature plants will produce spores, generally on the underside of the fronds. These spores have a dust-like appearance, either black or brown in colour, and are often mistaken for some form of disease. In some cases the spores appear on apparently disfigured fronds, which may be removed without any adverse effect on the fern.

> **Hint:** *Although some ferns are tender to severe cold – Cyathea spp. (tree ferns) for example – if the old fronds, once frosted, are folded over the growing point to protect the undeveloped new fronds they will readily regrow in the new growing season. These old fronds can be removed as the new growth begins to appear and fear of severe frost has passed.*

Some easy-to-grow ferns to liven up a cool, shady place outdoors are:

Cyathea australis and **C. brownii** – tall exotic tree ferns, reasonably fast

TOP: Rumohra adiantiformis, *the hardy, indigenous 'leather leaf' fern is a very adaptable fern for any garden.*

BOTTOM: *Holly fern (*Cyrtomium falcatum*) – a good low-light foliage plant.*

growing to 3–5 m tall and 3 m spread.

Cyathea capensis and **C. dregei** (now known as **Alsophila capensis** and **A. dregei**) are indigenous tree ferns; harder to find, slower growing, and do not spread quite as wide, but with time can grow to great heights – best left and enjoyed growing in their natural habitats.

Microlepia speluncae – a 60 cm tall, easy-to-grow, clump-forming fern.

Dicksonia antarctica – similar in appearance to a tree fern, yet smaller in width (1,5 m) and in height (3 m); can tolerate a reasonable amount of sun and is quite quick growing; ideal to plant in

the bare areas under mature tree ferns.

Cyrtomium falcatum (holly fern) – a 50 cm tall, large-leafed, glossy fern that easily adapts to outdoor conditions; indigenous, fast growing and an ideal filler in shady areas.

Rumohra adiantiformis (leather-leafed fern) – indigenous, 30–50 cm in height and easily grown if general fern-growing conditions are adhered to.

FERTILISER

All plants need to be fed, and as their roots move through the soil, absorbing all nutrients within reach, there is a need to replace these nutrients by way of assisted feeding.

Not all plant nutrients are absorbed by plants: rain leaches some nutrients through the soil particles beyond the reach of feeding roots, and in the case of containerised plants, watering flushes the nutrients out of the soil through the drainage holes of the container. Wherever roots reach, they deplete the nutritional value of the growing medium, as they progress away from the stem almost in line with the edge of the plant crown. The outer diameter of the plant, known as the 'drip line', is where most nutrients available in the medium are being absorbed by the plant, and this is the area of importance when feeding. Here nutrient deficiencies will cause the plant to react in one way or another, causing lack of flowers or fruit, yellowing of foliage, no new growth, stunted root development or, in the extreme, leaf drop and finally death.

To understand fertilisers it is necessary to understand plants' needs. Three major nutrients constitute the basis of general fertilisers. Their availability in general or specific fertilisers is represented by sets of three figures, e.g. 2:3:2 or 5:1:5.

The first figure represents the available nitrogen (N) in the composition. Nitrogen is largely responsible for the visible healthy growth of the plant, promoting good colour, vigorous growth and an abundance of foliage. Foliage plants require consistently high levels of nitrogen during the entire growing season, while other plants require this concentrated nitrogen as they push out new growth at the beginning of each new growing season. The higher the first number, the more nitrogen is included and available to the plant.

The middle figure represents phosphorus (P). As a separate fertiliser, this is known as superphosphates. It is generally used as an important single chemical because many inland areas lack sufficient natural phosphorus (phosphates), and more than the amount available in balanced

fertilisers needs to be applied. Phosphorus is essential for root development, flowering or fruiting and to ensure ripening of fruit or seeds.

The third figure represents available potassium (K). This is available as muriate of potash, or could be added by lightly scattering wood ash over the beds from time to time (not too much at any one time – 30 g per square metre). Potassium develops starches and sugars in plants and is essential for the proper development of fruit and vegetables, which build up large quantities of either sugar or starch. It is also needed to strengthen resistance to disease, and improve colour and flavour. Plants with a potassium deficiency are less able to tolerate cold weather and are thus more susceptible to frost damage (not that extra potassium will make a tender tropical plant easier to grow in frost areas, it won't; the plant will still be frosted).

There are numerous other elements that plants require in lesser quantities. These are called trace elements. Fortunately for the everyday gardener, it is no longer essential to know what role each of these elements play in the life, health and function of the plant. Fertiliser manufacturers have begun to clearly indicate on the container or bag the range of plants a particular product is designed to cater for. It's as simple as reading the label. For any trace element deficiencies that need to be corrected there are single trace elements available; or to take the guesswork out of trace element correction, a manufactured trace element mixture can be applied.

Fertilising should coincide with plants' growing seasons – i.e. August to April – although liquid fertilising of plants growing and flowering during winter would be advisable. Applications should be every six weeks – except when the fertiliser used states that it is a 'slow release' (SR) or 'controlled release' combination. In these cases, follow the application dates on containers. General rates of application should be 30–60 g per square metre. Do not over-feed; this can lead to plants being burnt. Rather feed less, more often.

Controlled release fertilisers are slowly released into the soil when the moisture and temperature levels are correct, allowing the gardener a fertilising-free period ranging from 3 to 18 months, depending on the design of a particular fertiliser. Each product usually has the feeding period on the container, e.g. 3–6 months. This means that after feeding at the beginning of a growing period, no further feeding is required until the beginning of the following growing season. Although limited, these products are increasing in popularity and more of them are appearing on the garden centre shelves.

It is wise to water well after feeding; this washes the fertiliser off the foliage onto the ground, and avoids small brown burn marks on the foliage, which are often mistaken as fungal problems. Don't feed larger areas than you can thoroughly water directly after feeding.

FROST
Obviously the first step to frost prevention is to plant material that can naturally withstand frost. Secondly, plant slightly tender material in positions that are protected by walls or

Frost damage on the tall, large leaves of Strelitzia nicolai *'Wild Banana'.*

other plants. Alternatively, if these plants can be grown in containers, do so, and move the containers to more protected areas during the winter months. Some plants are only tender when young, and able to withstand greater degrees of cold as they mature. These plants will need to be protected for their first couple of years. It is pointless to protect plants that are so sensitive that they frost each year, unless they can recover and grow to a respectable size during the following growing period. *Fuchsias* and daisy bushes are typical examples of such plants. They can be severely frosted, but if the base of the plant and the root system are protected with mulch or a loose packing of leaves, they will send out new growth, which will reach flowering size in the immediate growing season. Lastly, there are those plants that, once frosted, become naturally dormant until the beginning of the next growing season. Many ornamental grasses, water plants and perennials react in this way; this is natural and will occur each winter. It does not adversely affect the plant; in fact some plants (*Peonies* and *Astilbes*, for example) need that frost-induced dormant period to perform better the following year.

Protection of tender plants is best done with organic materials, as these generally do not conduct the low temperatures easily. Use materials such as hessian, veld grass bundles or cardboard. These are usually wrapped round the stem or entire plant. Try where possible to leave room for ventilation, or an opening in the covering on the northern side. Do not use plastic sheeting. A lightweight, synthetic, white fabric (available from garden centres) is simply draped over plants at night and removed during the warmer part of the morning.

Do not even attempt to protect the leaves unless the plant can safely be completely covered. A large enough cardboard box is ideal for this. The leaves will recover during the growing season; it is more important that the growing tip and stems are protected. In

the case of plants with large leaves that are normally frosted, such as tree ferns and wild bananas, do not remove the damaged leaves, simply fold them over the growing tips and leave in place until there are signs of new growth in spring.

> *Warning: It is not advisable to remove frosted foliage of any plants until the new growing season begins, as this often stimulates growth, which is re-frosted. This undermines the general strength of the plant.*

The correct timing of a watering programme can have an impact on the extent of any frost damage. Plants watered late in the afternoon, which are still wet when the temperatures begin do drop, are more susceptible to frosting than plants watered during the morning hours.

The term 'black frost' is given to the damage caused by below-freezing winds. There is very little that can be done to protect plants against this phenomenon, as the wind tends to blow into even the most protected corners. This drop of temperature and wind can occur at any time during the day or night and can easily catch the gardener unawares. Contrary to popular belief, there are no typical layers of frost; in fact, there are no visible symptoms other than the very low temperatures and wind.

FRUIT

Home fruit growing is not as popular as it used to be, but many properties have fruit trees established years ago, and new fruit trees are still being planted; both these and the old ones need to be cared for. Fruit trees fall into various groups:

ABOVE LEFT: Avocado, Persea americana, *a large tree for mild climate areas.*

ABOVE RIGHT: Citrofortunella x mitis *or Calamondin is a constant bearing, small edible or ornamental citrus.*

LEFT: Ideal for small spaces, plums need little pruning and they grow well in cold areas.

Tropical fruits

Avocado, guava, banana, kiwi-fruit, pecan, macadamia and paw-paw can be grown in some areas inland. Less successful are mango and litchi. Some of these fruit types need little space and can be tucked into protected areas. Others are large and will need careful positioning if they are to mature and bear fruit. Some, such as paw-paw and kiwi, need male and female plants to produce fruit. General feeding will be dealt with under soft fruit feeding.

Citrus

Although ostensibly tropical plants, these adapt well to colder areas and once established will bear fruit despite cold winters. Some citrus varieties perform better than others in cold areas. If choices must be made, lemons and oranges perform better than grapefruit and naartjies in most cold areas. Citrus plants grow well in containers and in extremely cold areas this is an alternative growing method to no citrus at all, particularly if fruit quantity is not a factor. Because citrus plants are evergreen, and flower and bear fruit in winter, they need to be watered and fed regularly during the winter months. Liquid foliar feeding is ideal for this type of feeding. General feeding will be dealt with under soft fruit feeding.

Soft fruits

Traditionally these are cold-climate fruit trees, deciduous and quick growing. They respond well to pruning, the fruits grow and ripen quickly, and the trees are extremely tolerant of cold, dry winters.

Cherries, peaches, apricots, plums, nectarines, apples and pears constitute the bulk of this fruit range although some oddities could be added, such as quinces, figs, pomegranates and cold climate nut trees such as almond, chestnut and walnut.

In past years these trees were planted in formal orchards, relegated to the 'back garden'. Some of them are still grown this way, and as they grow past their best fruit-bearing years, it is advisable to dig them out, to be replaced by new selected varieties, planted as small trees elsewhere in the garden. In this way new life can be brought to the orchard 'back garden', at the same time making the fruit tree a more versatile part of the whole garden.

The two major maintenance factors regarding these types of fruit trees are winter pruning and summer feeding.

Winter pruning

For many years the standard practice when pruning these trees was to open the centre, creating a 'wine glass'-shaped tree comprising 3–5 main branches off the central stem. Coupled to this was the tendency to keep the tree to a height that made for easy picking of fruit. Traditionally this shaped process was initiated by buying a 'whip', a tree that had been grown for one or two seasons after it had been grafted or budded. Once this tree had been planted with the bud or graft union just above ground level, the tree was cut off at knee height, or roughly 50 cm above the ground. During the following growing season the cut-off tree would develop young side branches.

In the first winter, in its permanent position, the strongest side branches, roughly 3–5 of them, evenly spaced round the central stem, were selected and the remainder removed. One third of their length was removed, cutting just above an outward-facing bud. Over several years of pruning, this resulted in the traditional 'cup' or 'wine glass' shape. More recently this has been simplified by fruit tree growers, who prune and prepare young fruit trees to the initial shaping stage before supplying these trees for sale.

Further annual pruning included removing all branches that grew inwards, crossed, were deformed or too thin to carry fruit. One third of the remaining growth was cut back to an outward-facing bud, and excess inner growth was removed to allow for sunlight and good ventilation. Fruiting wood was reduced by one third – again to an outside facing bud. (Buds that are most likely to bear flowers consist of a couple or more buds clustered together – single buds are usually leaf buds only.)

In past years all fruit trees were pruned; nowadays in the domestic garden situation, plums, apples, pears, cherries, figs, apricots and all deciduous nut trees are pruned to remove damaged and misshapen growth only. The reason for this is that the trees tend to grow too large or produce too much non-fruiting growth, too far above the general shape of the tree. Should there be a need to correct the shape of any of these types of fruit

Citrus reticulata or 'Naartjie', a well-known winter citrus for mild winter areas.

trees it would be best to employ an expert to prune them. Flowering fruit trees should be left to grow naturally, and not pruned as one would prune fruiting varieties.

More recently, domestic and commercial fruit tree pruning has become more adventurous. Trees are being grown closer together or against walls and frames. The pruning concepts have changed and in some cases are following the 'espalier' concepts followed in Europe. As these techniques are specialised, it is essential to attend demonstrations to see how the trees are treated from the beginning.

General feeding

Equally important for the setting of fruit is how the trees are fed, and when. During their growing period, and before, during and after crop harvesting, the trees need to be fed regularly, at least every six weeks, from August to April, in quantities related to the age of the tree. Fertiliser and superphosphates should be applied at a rate of 250 g of each per year of age, to a maximum of eight years. After this, the amount stays consistent at 2 kg per tree. Apply the fertilisers over the entire metre-wide band under the drip line. Should this be a grass-covered area, spike the lawn with a garden fork before applying the fertiliser.

If a tree should produce an over-abundance of fruit it is wise to thin out the crop by 25–30 per cent to ensure quality rather than poor quality in quantity.

Diseases of fruit trees

These are season-specific, in most cases affecting either foliage or fruit. Fungal, bacterial or viral diseases affecting trees can range from root rot or phytophthora, to canker, crown galls and various mildews or rusts. If attended to in the early stages, most diseases can be controlled with regular spraying. In severe cases, where the disease is either incurable – like crown gall – or too far advanced, the easiest solution is to remove and destroy the

tree or trees. This applies particularly to old trees and often coincides with crop returns so low that removal is not a major loss.

Some common fruit tree problems, which deserve mention:

Leaf curl on peaches – often as a result of early rains. The leaves curl, become swollen and disfigured, have an initial reddish colour but later turn yellow and often drop off. In severe cases young twigs and fruit can be affected with either a white, velvety 'bloom' or distortions. Crop losses can be expected. Winter spraying with lime sulphur or oil-based sprays, which are increasing in popularity as a means of control in winter, will help control this as well as hibernating pests hidden in the scaly mature bark.

Powdery mildew – affects new growth and fruit, covering both with a white powdery coating. Left unattended the twigs will die back and the fruit will become hard and cracks can appear. In severe cases the entire fruit will become covered with this coating and will not ripen. Spray as for leaf curl.

Crown gall appears as spherical nodules at soil level or just below it. This

cannot be cured and removal of the tree is recommended. Do not plant another similar tree in the same area.

Some apparent diseases are often caused by physical problems. This is the case with sunburn, resulting in the bark cracking and flaking off. Sunburn is caused by over-pruning the centre of the fruit tree and exposing the bark, which is damaged by the sun. Similarly, over-bearing (too many young fruit are set), snap frost, dry spells or excessive transpiration on hot, dry, windy days can cause fruit to drop and leaves to become scarred. Ripening fruit often cracks when, after a dry spell, there is a lot of rain or excessive watering. The skin of the fruit hardens during the dry spell, then cannot expand with the amount of moisture available and cracks.

Dieback (phytophthora) can be particularly active in poorly drained soil in summers when the rainfall is abnormally high. Whole branches (or whole older trees) can steadily die off. Remove the trees and replant new trees in better-drained areas. A similar effect can be seen on citrus trees, where over-watering causes the bark at the base of the tree to rot and leaves to yellow; gum is exuded and finally the tree dies.

Strawberries are easy to grow, either in rows, at random in the garden as a ground cover, or in an attractive strawberry barrel.

Viral or fungal infestations can cause large areas of the bark on citrus trees to die and flake off. As a result the tree often has dieback-like symptoms before it dies.

Pests of fruit trees

Generally, on soft fruit types, apples, pears and some nut varieties, fruit flies are the most common problem, 'stinging' the fruit at a young stage and laying their eggs in the undeveloped fruit. As the fruit matures, so too do the maggots, causing the fruit to rot as it ripens, and drop off. This fallen fruit should be disposed of, as the maggots it contains will hibernate in the soil and re-emerge as a mature fly in the new season. Control, either environmental or chemical, must be at the petal drop stage, before the fruit forms. Several tried and tested chemical controls are available and various environmental methods have been suggested. See PESTS.

Pear slug is a common problem that affects fruiting and ornamental plums as well as pears, cherries and apple trees in the latter part of the growing season. A black, shiny, tadpole-like slug eats the leaves, until only the vein network of the leaf is left. There are approved sprays on the market to combat this pest, but if possible, during the winter months, cultivate the soil under the affected trees as this helps to expose the hibernating pupae, which then die. If cultivation is not possible, spray the ground under the tree when spraying the tree.

The majority of pests are active as the fruit ripens. To control birds, use a bird net or cotton wound over the lower half of the tree. This means that they will only have access to fruit ripening on the upper parts of the tree. Fruit beetles can be controlled by hand picking, biological control methods or suitable contact poisons.

Other pests on various fruit types can range from slugs, centipedes and beetles on strawberries, to large green caterpillars on citrus and vine foliage, and rodents, monkeys (and children!) on any ripening fruit almost anywhere as the seasons advance. For all of these problems various methods of control are available and it is advisable to ask reliable garden centre staff what is new, safer or environmentally friendly before any seasonal purchases.

Vines

The fruit most praised in poetry and music, and justifiably so; the fruit of the vine is the source of the world's wine and some good home-made wines too. Equally important are the varieties grown for table grapes, some of which have been bred particularly for the domestic garden. Make sure when selecting a vine that it will grow well in the designated area. Few vines that grow well in the winter rainfall regions of the Cape will grow well in summer rainfall areas.

Pruning a vine is specific to the manner in which it is to grow and develop, and expert advice should be called in to set the pruning trend in the right direction.

Other fruit types

These range from all the berry types, such as blackberries, strawberries, raspberries, blueberries ... to Cape gooseberries and a whole range of odd ones in between. As each one of these has its own growth pattern (many of the 'berry' family can be quite invasive), methods of pruning and feeding and specifics regarding position, it is advisable to gather information regarding the specific fruit and its needs before planting. Some could serve as a groundcover; the 'berry' types could be relegated to a screen or fence.

Passiflora edulis 'Grenadilla', *a semi-tender short-lived climber.*

All figs, Ficus carica, *require lots of water when fruit begins to develop.*

Quince, great for jam and preserves, make an ideal spring flowering screen.

FUNGI

Generally awareness of fungi in the garden is directed at the types that have adverse effects on the condition or appearance of plants. Common fungi include:

Black spot initially appears as pale yellow blotches on foliage, which as the disease progresses turn black in the centre surrounded by yellowing. Finally, if these leaves are left unattended, they will turn completely yellow with black blotches of various sizes and fall off. Control is with an appropriate fungicide designed to control black spot.

White (or powdery) mildew affects a number of different plants. It appears as a flour-like dusting on foliage, stalks and unopened flower buds. If left unattended, the mildew will cause the foliage or buds to become deformed, shrivelled, finally dying off. Systemic fungicides help to control this, but regular seasonal spraying will be necessary, especially in times of warm, wet weather.

Peach leaf curl is a leaf-disfiguring fungus that attacks new peach foliage, enlarging the leaf at the same time as it curls it into a disfigured form. These affected leaves will finally fall off and new foliage will be produced. For control: see Diseases of fruit trees on page 30.

Various rusts, which appear as brown, black or orange spots on the either the upper or underside of the leaves, initially appear as small blisters that break open, looking like small spots of 'rust'. These 'blisters' increase in number and size until the entire leaf is covered and deformed and dies. Combat with appropriate fungicides. If the plants are known to be affected in warm, wet weather, spraying the plants with contact sprays before infestation will help keep them healthy.

In some cases there are few distinct outward indications other than wilting or dying off of foliage, new growing tips, flowers or the entire plant. These fungi attack the root system of the plants or the soft tissue of the stem at ground level.

Minute spores, often wind- or water-borne, carry all these common fungal-based problems, as well as many others. All of them are akin to mushrooms, toadstools and other fungi that attack rotting and decaying vegetation.

All fungi have dual growth – that which appears on or under the surface of the affected plant, and the mycelium or 'root system', which is embedded in the plant cells. For complete control it is important that systemic fungicides are used, which work up from the root system into the plant cells. Systemic fungicides are not washed off by watering or rain, and as a result have a more lasting effect. This is particularly the case with plants such as English oak and pride of India, which suffer badly from a form of powdery mildew. Surface or contact sprays are ideal in cases where prevention is intended *before* the symptoms are apparent. This prevents windborne spores from attaching themselves to the plant.

As fungi thrive in humid, warm, overcast or dark conditions, the wet summer months are their most prevalent period. Plants that are known to be vulnerable to fungi should be sprayed regularly at this time of the year. This is essential, as the spores will continue to mature and drift during these ideal climatic conditions and susceptible plants will be constantly at risk. Plants that are adversely affected should be grown in drier, more sunny parts of the garden, or in the case of some annuals and perennials, either grown during the drier months or in less crowded positions, where ventilation between plants keeps them dry. Plants such as *Zinnia*, *Hydrangea*, roses, English oak, pride of India and perennial *Phlox* are regularly affected, and – prevention being better than cure – should be sprayed from early summer to early autumn to keep them healthy.

The simplest defence against fungus is to select plants that are not readily affected, limit the problem plants to the minimum, or plant them together in areas where collective spraying is easy.

To further prevent fungus from developing, do not water at sunset if the air is warm and humid. Fungus develops rapidly in the night hours if moisture is present and temperatures and humidity are high. It would appear that this applies particularly to the development of lawn grass fungi. If watering is done earlier the heat can help evaporate the moisture on the foliage whilst it is still daylight.

In soils that retain a lot of moisture, and 'damping off' of seedlings and young perennials occurs, either improve the drainage by adding coarse drainage material (e.g. sand, power station ash or fine gravel), or water the area with a root rot and 'damping-off' fungicide before planting out the young plants or sowing the seed.

GRASS

A variety of grasses, each with its own specific uses, growing habits and requirements, are used to create domestic lawns.

Facts about lawn grasses

- Most grasses will be tolerant of either sun or shade; few are equally at home in both.

- There are cool- or warm-season grasses. Cool-season grasses are more evergreen than the warm-season grasses, many of which are dormant or 'frosted off' in the winter months.

- Grasses are propagated from runners (stolons or rhizomes) or seed. In some cases the better varieties can be purchased as instant sod, grown and harvested on grass farms.

- Lawn is a living plant and needs to be cared for as such: this means regular feeding, watering and mowing during its growing period.

- In areas where there is regular traffic, no living plant will withstand wear as readily as grass – *but* no grass will withstand heavy regular traffic.

- Some lawn grasses need more care than others, and the cost of maintaining these areas can be prohibitively high.

- When mowing any grass type, no more than one third of the foliage growth should be removed at a time.

- Cool-season or tufted grasses – commonly called evergreen or seed lawn grasses, should not be cut as short as warm-season or runner grasses – it can safely be said that these grass types should be at least 5–6 cm tall after they have been cut. They can be allowed to grow taller to give a 'meadow' appearance.

- Tufted grass types will seldom withstand the urine of dogs – it

A well-maintained 'cool season' lawn sown from seed.

causes patches that will yellow and die off. This can often be confused with lawn grass diseases. (A small area of the same lawn grown elsewhere, in a dog-free zone, which can be dug out as small sods to fill in such areas will help; alternatively, keep a supply of seed handy to sow into these patches when needed

- Lawn grasses, both runner and tufted types, have specific seasonal requirements if they are to be kept in peak condition. These are not simply feeding, cutting and watering, but more specific and relative to each lawn type. Top-dressing, scarifying, and aerating or hollow-tineing are examples of specialist seasonal lawn care practices.

- It is not essential to top-dress lawn each year – only if there is levelling to be done. Never top-dress tufted, cool-season seed lawns; they will die if covered with top dressing.

- When establishing a lawn by means of seed, apply seed at the suggested rate. Don't reduce the rate per square metre and don't try to make the seed 'stretch' further than recommended – the result will be patchy.

- Deciduous, warm-season grasses need a winter rest period. It is not wise to try and keep them 'green' through this period. (Over-seeding these lawns in winter with a cool-season grass is an alternative, but perhaps too specialised for the home garden.)

- Different grass types have different applications. Using the correct grass in the appropriate situation will reduce maintenance.

Cool-season grasses

These are mainly grasses raised from seed: they are tufted (no runners), evergreen and tolerant of extremely cold conditions. Most of them are sold under brand names registered to seed suppliers, and new varieties or mixtures are constantly being tested for the South African market. If they are to be sown from seed, the ideal times are spring and autumn, when germination is

Warm-season 'kikuyu' lawn must have lots of sun and attention to look its best.

better. Winter is too cold, and summer in most areas too hot. If the grass is available as instant sods or rolls of grass, these can be laid at any time of the year.

Some of these grass types are mixtures, which makes them more suitable in many situations than the single-seed types. The mixed seed makes allowances for variations in growing conditions or positions, whereas the single-seed types may not perform well with no alternative backup. Any of them will be ideal for a small area or where consistent detail is required. Maintenance of tufted grasses is generally easier than runner-type grasses; however they do need regular watering in dry periods and regular mowing, albeit less often than traditional runner type lawns. Because they do not produce runners, edging is a simple task. With either a lawn edge trimmer or shears, perfect edges can be maintained for a considerable length of time. If contained within a form of lawn edging, a sharp knife or spade will suffice.

Some cool-season grasses are intended to grow in shade, others in

sun, and some are said to grow equally well in both sun and shade. Check the information on the container before sowing.

There are fine-bladed and coarse-bladed varieties available to add to and blend in with existing lawn areas where warm-season grasses will not grow. It is essential, when preparing a seed bed for sowing, to ensure that the area is level. This is because once the seed has germinated, these grass types cannot be top-dressed. This will also apply to the method of laying sod – they must be accurately placed with no gaps, as they cannot spread out and cover these spaces.

Warm-season grasses

Typically, most of these lawn types produce stolons, rhizomes or runners, which root as they grow along or under the ground. This means that if they are left unattended they can encroach onto pathways or into flowerbeds. Maintenance of these grasses can be high.

The fine-leafed varieties, such as 'Bay view', 'Gulf Green', 'Richmond', 'Florida' or 'Cape Royal' are all sun-loving grasses of indigenous origin. Generally tolerant of drought and cold conditions, they are ideal alternatives to the more vigorous, invasive kikuyu, and equally at home in small and large areas. They are reasonably disease free, only needing regular watering during the hot, dry, growing season before and after the mid-season rains. All of them are dormant during winter. All will tolerate being mown less often than kikuyu, will respond well to regular feeding but in rugged areas will survive well with little or no attention. Sadly, all of these grasses are less 'extreme traffic tolerant' than kikuyu.

The broad-bladed warm-season grass of choice is kikuyu. This sun-loving, water-thirsty, greedy feeder requires a lot of maintenance. It is highly invasive, which makes it suitable only for large areas, but despite this it is still the most widely planted lawn in the country. Kikuyu has its positive aspects too; it is extremely hard-wearing, quick to cover and recover, almost totally disease-free and adaptable to a wide range of climatic conditions. **Kikuyu dislikes damp, cold shade**. This is why it will not grow in deep shade of plants and dies off against the south side of walls, houses or shrubberies. It also dislikes growing in the areas where swimming pool backwash is pumped out.

Other broad-bladed warm-season grasses, such as 'LM', 'Buffalo', 'Swazi' and 'St. Augustine', are more area-specific in terms of their sun/shade preferences as well as their climatic requirements. Seasonal care of these grasses is simple: cut when necessary (never more than one third of the blade length), and feed during the growing period (every six weeks from August to May). If there is no rain, water well before and after fertilising. Don't feed areas too large to water thoroughly afterwards.

Remove the build-up of dead grass (thatch) during the dormant period, just before the new growing season; this is part of what is commonly called 'spring-treatment'. Spike compacted areas every two to three years, in August, before feeding. Top-dress (only if necessary) in early spring. Water the area *before* top-dressing and not after – until the new grass blades push through the *dry*, sifted top-dressing.

Hint: Do not apply top dressing too thick, rather in thinner layers, allowing time in between for grass to grow through it each time.

Keep lawnmower blades sharp to provide a clean cut. If the mower is a cylinder or 'drum' type, make sure the cutting space between the bottom blade and cylinder blades is set correctly to cut with a close 'scissor' action. (It should be possible to cut paper!)

Feeding grass

Feed every six weeks, from early August to mid-May, with a general, balanced fertiliser such as 3:1:5, or a balanced fertiliser designed specifically to feed grass (4:1:1). Either can be applied at the rate of 60 g per square metre. Make sure the ground is wet both before and after feeding to prevent burning the grass. If it is necessary to feed with LAN (limestone ammonium nitrate), apply sparingly, in between general feeding. Don't feed too early in the season with LAN, preferably from mid-October onwards, when grass is growing well and remember to water thoroughly after applying it to avoid burning. Remember LAN only produces foliage growth and improved colour – it doesn't feed the grass, but it can burn it. If possible, apply fertilisers with a fertiliser spreader, which applies the granules evenly, avoiding overlapped applications that result in burning.

Lawn pests and diseases

Crickets, mole crickets, harvester ants and lawn caterpillars are generally the only pests that readily destroy lawn (apart from the occasional dog or similar pest digging up a patch just for the fun of it!) All can be controlled with available products – or consider environmental alternatives, such as flushing the holes as they become obvious, with soapy water, or water with diluted Jeyes fluid – 5 tablespoons per 10 litres of water in areas where pests are active.

Fungal diseases will establish themselves on grasses if conditions are ideal – a thick thatch of dead grass, warm damp weather, watering too late in the afternoon during the warmer months, weak unfed grass. Most diseases are readily controlled with lawn fungicides. Generally their symptoms are yellowing and subsequently small dead patches, which enlarge if not treated. Similar symptoms are evident when dogs urinate on grass. In this case the grass will begin to re-grow if watered well. On seed lawns this area will die off totally and will need to be replaced.

Mushrooms can be a problem, growing in a 'fairy ring' of bright green grass. The ring expands with each season and the inner part of the circle is left under-nourished. Mushrooms and 'toadstools' are the visible parts of a fungal growth and can be controlled with a systemic fungicide.

Prevention is better than cure. Water early in the day so that the grass blades dry before sunset. Remove thatch build-up in winter. Keep lawn well fed, regularly. Treat mushroom appearances and irregular yellow patches immediately with fungicide.

Lawn weeds

Most lawn areas are infested with weeds from time to time. Weeds are wind-borne or spread by lawnmowers, birds, animals, or on the soles of shoes. They will become a problem where the grass is poorly matted – either because it was not planted or sown thick enough, underfed or not suitable for the area. A gap in grass is where weeds will germinate and grow.

Control of weeds

Manually remove the weeds, either one at a time or, in areas that are densely infested, by digging out the entire area and replacing with new weed-free sods.

Spray with a **selective** herbicide (weed killer) designed to control specific weeds in lawns. There are several to choose from, and applying the wrong one will be a costly mistake. Make sure the product purchased will eradicate only the specific weeds, which should be identified before buying the herbicide.

Often winter is an ideal time to weed dormant lawns, as the weeds are obvious and easily removed or sprayed.

Apply controlled 'spot' treatment with **non-selective** glysophate-based weed killers. Remember that these will kill anything green, if application is too haphazard. They are ideal herbicides where areas of persistent weed growth defeat even the most ardent attempts at eradication by any other method. Glysophate-based herbicides can be applied as a spray, painted on with a brush or dabbed on with a sponge.

Lastly, if the weed is not unsightly, ignore it and mow along with the grass.

GROUNDCOVERS

Groundcovers are used to cover the ground in any situation where grass is not not practical or visually appealing. Their vigour, height, growing conditions and requirements vary, making some of the plants more suitable in some situations and not in others.

Facts about groundcovers

- Some groundcovers are suited for use in large areas, others for small.

- Some groundcovers simply cover an area by way of their spread, known as clump forming; these plant types are best used on level areas as they do not readily prevent erosion or retain banks.

- Other ground-covering plants are spread by runners and root as they grow, finally covering large areas. These are the ideal plants for covering ground, as they can retain banks and prevent soil erosion. Moreover, their runners can be trained into less favourable areas whilst their roots grow in more favourable positions.

- Groundcovers cannot take the wear and tear that grass can and are used in areas where grass would not be practical. If there is regular traffic across groundcovers, use stepping-stones set among them.

- Do not mix vigorous groundcovers suited for large areas, with less vigorous types more suited to small areas, as they will be overgrown.

> *Hint: Do not plant groundcovers too far apart: aim at covering the ground as quickly as possible. This applies particularly to clump-forming plants. Vigorous and large plants: 3–5 per square metre Slow and smaller plants: 9–11 per square metre Small clump plants that do not run: 15 per square metre.*

- Some groundcovers need to be split up and replanted every 3–5 years to maintain good coverage.

- Overgrown groundcovers can be cut down once a year with a lawnmower or edging machine.

- Mulch with compost early in the growing season; wash the compost off the foliage into the root area.

- Use plastic edging or something similar to separate different groundcovers; cut along this edge to keep groundcovers separated.

- Vigorous groundcovers will need regular balanced fertilising as well as regular pruning to keep them contained within their intended areas.

- Some groundcovers are not affected by garden pests, but harbour them. This is often the case with such pests as slugs, snails and aphids – even though the plants are not eaten, it is a good idea to spray or dust them with an insecticide or bait to keep the pests under control.

- Groundcovers that are eaten can be dusted with a systemic granular insecticide, as indicated.

- Rodents are kept at bay with rodent blocks, traps, and in smaller areas, by spraying with a khakibos solution – one bucket rough chopped khakibos plants and two buckets boiling water, mix in a large drum, stand overnight, strain, add a half cup dishwashing liquid soap and spray on areas of activity.

- Some groundcovers, such as *Gazanias* and 'vygies', are susceptible to fungal infestation, causing dying-off of foliage in the centres of plants. Treat with systemic fungicides at first signs of yellowing or dying foliage. These groundcovers generally need to be lifted, split and replanted from time to time to keep a healthy covering of the area.

The multi-coloured contrast from some groundcovers breathes new life into open spaces in the garden beds.

HEDGES

There was a time in garden design when almost every home had a hedge, clipped and kept in pristine condition. Then the cost of labour, time spent in trimming, the rising cost of hedging plants and the advent of the pre-cast concrete wall made it lose its popularity to open-plan gardens (no surrounds at all) or more informal shrubberies. Recently, however, the hedge has begun to feature in gardens again, but with specific demands both from the plant type used and the role of the hedge.

Hedges have become almost an art form, lining pathways, edging formal plantings or ponds, as screens alongside a swimming pool or patio and as interesting dividers of the garden space. Some are only centimetres tall, while others are above average head height. Irrespective of the size intended, there are specific pointers that will not only ensure their success, but their lifespan and performance too.

- Select plants that will respond to regular pruning. Plant them no further apart than is necessary for them to comfortably expand into each other, within a reasonable time span, without gaps or overcrowding.

- Should the proposed hedge be low and narrow (less than 50 cm high or wide) plant the plants roughly 30 cm apart. Select plants that would not naturally grow too tall or be too vigorous.

- For medium-sized hedges, between 50 cm and 120 cm tall x 50 cm wide, plant the plants 50–60 cm apart.

- For tall hedges, 120 cm and taller, and wider than 50 cm, plant the plants one metre apart. Large shrubs, conifers and small trees will suffice for this size hedge.

- Once new growth appears, do not leave the plants too long before starting to give regular **light** clippings. This will force the plant to begin branching repeatedly from near ground level and from an early age.

- As the plants begin to touch each other, there are several ways that the hedge can be formed. If it is to remain low and narrow, a template can be cut out of hardboard, the final size and shape of the hedge. This is moved along the row of plants, and anything growing outside the template shape is cut off.

Manageable-sized formal hedges can be set out within metal rods, which are knocked into position at corners, angles and through any curves – spaced 50 cm apart. These rods are knocked in until all are at the desired hedge height. Thin wires are strung from rod to rod at the required height. The plants are regularly clipped in line with these wires.

The more conventional method used in the recent past, was simply to vertically trim the plants to a desired height and cut them flat on the top. However, more recently hedge creators have begun to reconsider a practice from centuries past – the tapered hedge, trimmed narrower as it moved upwards. This form of clipping allows the lower foliage to receive as much light as the foliage higher up on the plants, ensuring that there is even foliage cover all over the plants. The inward slope is slight; no more than a few degrees from vertical.

Clipped low hedges add a touch of classic formality to any garden.

Problems that can be encountered when growing hedges

- Pests and diseases particular to the plant chosen can become a serious problem because of the number of plants used, their close proximity and the dense growth caused by regular clipping. Control can prove to be long term and difficult, because the pests and diseases can move from plant to plant.

- Insect problems such as red spider mite, scale and mealy bug or woolly aphid can become intense, as they are seldom seen until infestation is advanced. This is due to the density of foliage.

- Should disease or pests cause plants to die off, it is difficult to replace these plants with new material and expect it to 'catch up' to the density and size of the other plants.

- Incorrect clipping can result in the hedge becoming 'woody', leafless, and 'open', with all the foliage near the top, which reduces screening capacity.

- Hedges tend to create their own microclimate. This often results in the area drying out, creating too much shade on the south side, and depleting the soil. Left unattended, these aspects can cause the hedge to lose vigour, die off or grow sparsely. Regular feeding will help, but if the plant cannot tolerate dry conditions or shade it will begin to deteriorate.

A popular alternative to the true clipped hedge is to establish a 'tapestry' hedge consisting of a selection of plants with similar growing habits, but different foliage, flowering seasons and colour variations. These plants can be planted at reasonable distances apart, depending on their final size, and clipped to the desired height and width. Because each chosen plant will have different growing requirements, they will be less affected by common disease and pest problems. An oriental variation on this theme is to clip each type of plant to reflect its individual needs and characteristics, creating interest with the various plants and heights. This is called 'cloud hedging', because of its likeness to a bank of storm clouds.

Privacy and formality are provided with tidy hedge planting.

Informal hedging is a simple solution to many typical hedge problems. Plants are planted close enough to meet and create the desired hedge; however, they are seldom clipped, and if clipping is necessary, it is usually to remove damaged, dead and misshapen material. Plants chosen for this type of hedge must be selected with care, considering their density, rate of growth, distance apart, seasonal behaviour and their ability to grow in close proximity with other plants. More space is needed to grow this type of hedge.

HERBACEOUS BORDERS

Long regarded as the ideal way to display perennials, providing a wide range of colour throughout the year, the herbaceous border was more a European concept than one common to South Africa. However, during the last decade the introduction of suitable plant material has made it more popular. The secret to a successful herbaceous border is knowing the

Herbaceous borders can be small and detailed (above) or large and massed (overleaf).

specific growing requirements of each plant type used. Though traditionally formal in shape, the areas chosen for a herbaceous border can be any size, and informal if necessary.

The border would be designed around a few well-chosen specimen plants, such as standard flowering or foliage plants. These would be formally or informally used, depending on the overall effect desired.

- Sub-shrubs and focal shrubs would contribute to the colour scheme of the planting; roses, lavender, rosemary, daisy bushes, etc. could be added to provide permanent height and structure. Sub-shrubs are shrubs that are generally cut back to ground level from time to time to encourage new growth (they flower on new or soft growth). This prevents the plant from becoming too woody (filled with old wood) such as *Fuchsia*, *Streptosolen*, *Argyranthemum*, *Cerastostigma* and *Lavandula*.

- Evergreen perennials, such as *Iris*, hellebores, *Agapanthus*, day lilies, *Acanthus*, ferns, Cape thatch grasses, etc. could be grown for foliage as well as flowers.

- Deciduous perennials would contribute to the overall effect during specific seasons, e.g. *Cannas* (summer), Michaelmas daisy (autumn), *Peonies* (spring), *Liliums* (various), *Chrysanthemums* (autumn), and so on.

- Ornamental grasses are ideal plants to use for varied shape, colour and texture as well as seasonal contrast.

- Annuals and biennials include foxgloves, *Dianthus*, sweet William, hollyhocks, sunflowers, *Alyssum*, etc.

- Self-seeding plants are ideal for this colour effect – *Alyssum*, marigold, *Primula*, nasturtium, *Linaria*, honesty, and such like.

- Herbs and vegetables such as spinach, lettuce, parsley, and fennel can add effective short-term foliage contrasts.

- The overall effect is one of semi-permanence, with points of interest changing with the seasons.

- They can be based on specific colour schemes and foliage effects, or can be a random collection of plants grown for foliage and colour.

> **Hint:** *For the ideal visual effect, make sure that there are sufficient numbers of each plant. The smaller the individual plant, the more will need to be used, and, by the same token, fewer of the larger plants.*

Allow space for the perennial material to multiply and expand for several years, without overcrowding the planting. Allow seasonal space for such vigorous plants as shasta daisy, *Chrysanthemum*, *Dahlia* and *Canna*. Remember that some plants grow outwards as they grow upwards – ornamental grasses, *Acanthus* and ferns, for example – and provide sufficient space for their mature effect.

Pests and diseases would be general and typical and will be dealt with under their own headings.

Feeding must be constant: typically an application of general balanced fertiliser and superphosphates needs to be applied every six weeks at the rate of 60 g per square metre, with a liquid organic fertiliser applied every 10 days, especially during the flowering period.

HERBS

Perhaps the most popular aspect of gardening today. Herbs

CLOCKWISE FROM TOP LEFT: An annual basil variety, leaves are great for pesto and salads, Nigella seed for extra flavour and lemon balm, Melissa officinalis, leaves to add a tang of lemon to a salad.

are grown for their value in the kitchen, as herbal remedies, for their aroma or scent, and simply for the old world charm they represent.

Important: All herbs must grow in full sun to realise their full potential.

Herbs fall into several botanical categories. When making a selection, consider the growing character of each plant **before** planting. This helps to avoid mistakes with height, spread and seasonal performance.

Annual – Many of these are grown for their seed, e.g. dill, coriander, aniseed and cumin. Others are grown for leaves or flowers – basil, borage and *Nasturtium*.

Biennial – These plants grow for two years, flowering, seeding and dying in their second year. Grown for seed, flowers, roots or leaves; they are either used green, e.g. parsley and *Angelica*, or allowed to set seed, then harvested, e.g. caraway.

Perennial – An on-going plant, though in some cases the seasonal growth dies off in the winter months and reappears in August. There are those such as mint and tarragon, which spread widely by way of underground runners or stolons. These need containers or large areas where they can expand. Chives, garlic, horseradish and shallots are often dug up, harvested and young side shoots or bulblets (sets) are replanted to grow for another season. Rosemary, thyme, fennel, sage, lemon balm and dandelion need to be cut back regularly – this happens when harvesting. Herbal shrubs such as rose, bay, juniper, jasmine and myrtle are treated like any other shrub in the garden and pruned if and when necessary.

All herbs should be fed regularly and watched for insects. Like vegetables and fruit, they should be sprayed with deterrents rather than killer chemicals.

Herbs are seldom affected by fungal problems, but it is important that they are grown in well-composted, well-drained soil to avoid root rot and damping off.

Most herbs will grow well in containers as long as the above soil requirements are adhered to. Do not overcrowd the containers; rather have several different containers with fewer plants in them. Their need for good sunlight may lead to containers drying out, so water well and regularly. In the case of dormant perennials such as mint, do not allow the stolons to dry out during the dry winter months.

Herbs do not need to be planted in a specific place and can happily combine with annuals, general perennials, in shrubberies or as insect deterrents in vegetable areas. Many well-known herbs are ideal companion plants, enhancing the general health, flavour and growth of plants growing near them.

Chillies in a whole range of colours, shapes – and hotness!

See list, COMPANION PLANTING.

Harvesting herbs

Flowers and leaves should be collected either early morning or late afternoon. If these are to be dried, do not allow them to touch one another and dry them on racks in a cool dry place. If used fresh, pick flowers when the flower is mature but not fully blown. Leaves should be harvested when mature, before the flowering period of the plant.

If **stems and branches** are cut, cut often rather than too severely. Don't cut into areas of the plant that are bare leafless stems. Harvest leaves and stems before the plant flowers, and dry them bunched upside down in paper packets – don't use plastic bags. Hang in cool dry area to dry – The garage is often an ideal place.

Seed harvesting begins when the seed begins to change colour from green to yellow-green or brown. If the plant is annual, remove the entire plant, tie the heads into a large paper bag, and hang the plants upside down until the seed matures and falls off. If the plant is not removed, cut the seed-bearing stems and dry them on a tray or in a paper bag. Take care – some seeds 'jump' as their capsules ripen and scatter their seeds.

Fruit harvesting

- Nasturtium – harvest seeds when young and soft inside, soon after the flower falls apart. Use fresh or pickled.
- *Sambucus*/elder – harvest berries when fully ripe and black. Use fresh for jelly, sauce, wine or freeze for sauces.
- Rose hips – before the hips shrivel and harden. Use fresh or dried.
- Pomegranate – when the outside of the fruit is red and beginning to crack open. Use fresh.
- Chillies and peppers – either when green for mild flavour or when deep red for stronger flavour. Use green as fresh or frozen fruit, red can be used fresh or dried.

Roots of horseradish are harvested when dormant in winter. Thin roots, too small to clean and scrape, are replanted. Use fresh, frozen or pickled. Tops of root with dormant shoots can be cut off and rooted for replanting. Other roots such as angelica or fennel should be harvested at the end of the growing season and used fresh.

Bulbs – mostly garlic and shallots – are harvested when leaves die off. The leaves are tied together and the bunch hung in a cool, dry place to dry. Shallots are perennial and need not be lifted. Use fresh, pickled or as a vinegar or oil flavouring.

> *Hint: Some herbs – e.g. basil, chives, garlic chives and French tarragon – do not keep well when dried and should be used fresh or made into a pesto with oil.*

It is not wise to harvest too much from one plant: if it is a popular herb, plant more than one. In the case of biannuals such as parsley, plant new plants annually to ensure that there is a constant supply of usable foliage.

When herbs are harvested for use in medicinal preparations it is important that the material is disease-free, fresh, in optimum condition, and dry. Do not harvest after watering or rain, but allow the plants to dry naturally before harvesting. They should be hygienically dried (in paper bags), quickly, in well-ventilated, cool places and used as soon as thoroughly dry.

INDOOR PLANTS

No plant evolved growing in containers, indoors. All indoor plants, no matter what type, are growing in artificial conditions. To provide these plants with the near ideal conditions in which to grow and develop into mature plants, specific attention must be given to various aspects of their growth.

Indoor plants loosely fall into several categories:

Seasonal flowering plants – Often annual, but some perennials are included in this category. *Chrysanthemums*, *Cineraria*, *Primula*, *Calceolaria* and poinsettia are among the plants marketed as flowering indoor plants. They are regarded as disposable once they have finished flowering.

Perennial flowering plants – Generally plants with attractive foliage, which flower as well, e.g. African violets, *Spathiphyllum*, eucaris lilies, *Streptocarpus*, *Hoya*, some *Begonias* and succulents or cacti. They are generally repotted, but kept healthy by regular feeding.

Seasonable foliage plants – Plants such as *Coleus*, *Fittonia*, *Begonia*, *Caladium* and *Dieffenbachia* are regarded as short-

CLOKWISE: Potted Chrysanthemums, *African violets,* New Guinea Impatiens *and* Coleus *are all excellent colourful, short-lived indoor plants.*

term foliage effect material. Although some of these plants are perennial, they react badly to drops in temperature during winter and seldom recover well.

Perennial foliage material – This is the largest category of indoor plants. Mostly tropical, and grown to survive various indoor conditions, they can live to become mature plants with feeding, replanting and general care.

Irrespective of which plants are chosen, there are factors that have to be considered when a plant is purchased and placed indoors:

Light
Each plant needs a specific range of light intensity to enable it to grow properly. Light intensity is measured in units of *lux*. This is similar to the light readings of a camera and is measured with a meter. It is not necessary to own such a meter to correctly position an indoor plant, but it is important to know what light level the plant would prefer. Analyse the various rooms, which way windows face, when and how far sunlight penetrates into the room. It is important to remember that not all plants need the same lux levels; some are tolerant of very low levels of light, while others need high light levels. Light intensity is a major contributing factor to successful plant growth.

Air circulation
There is a decided difference between good air circulation and a draughty position, between air-conditioned and natural air flow. Air temperature and humidity levels also have their effects on the condition of indoor plants. Too high a level of humidity without air circulation will result in plants that are readily affected by fungal diseases. If the air is too dry (passed through an air conditioner), the foliage will dry out at the edges and form discoloured markings.

Temperature
Extreme air temperature and rapid changes in air temperatures will also have adverse effects on plants. Plants sensitive to cold will show signs of stress – dropping of leaves, discoloration of foliage, watery soft growth – and stems, leaves, or entire plants will appear to be 'frosted'. If the area is too hot, growth becomes elongated, sensitive to disease, often pale in colour and suffering from lack of water (moisture in containers evaporates quicker and plants transpire quicker). Extreme temperature changes cause similar situations – drying out of foliage, dropping of leaves, flowers die off quickly: these symptoms are often experienced in rooms where heaters are used during the evenings. Cold draughts will damage foliage and in some sensitive plant situations, cause the plant to die off partially or completely.

> *Hint: To create artificial humidity during the dry winter months, stand a bowl of water in between potted plants or make sure that the drip trays are regularly filled with water. If a humidifier is available this will help in rooms filled with several plants.*

Containers for indoor plants
Some indoor plants enjoy limited growing space, and are quite content to grow in small, restrictive containers. African violets, palms and some cacti and succulents are typical of these. Others will not need large containers, as they are expected to have a limited lifespan, and the original

Add a touch of foliage colour and the right container to liven up even the smallest of spaces indoors.

container is ideal for this time span – *Chrysanthemums* and *Azaleas*, for example. Slow-growing plants will live for several seasons in the same container, because their root system will not regularly require a larger amount of growing medium. This is the case with some orchids, ferns and bromeliads.

In many typical cases, however, the plant will finally require repotting (see CONTAINERS).

Watering indoor plants
More indoor plants are killed by incorrect watering than by any other means – either too much too often, or too little too seldom. Ideally, water only as the plant requires it – either the surface of the growing medium has dried out or the drip tray is empty. This, in most typical indoor situations, would be every 5–7 days; perhaps more often if the plant stands in a sunny position. A cool shady position will result in the plant requiring less water less often. Check the following:

- How long does the surface take to dry out?
- Does the plant wilt quickly in its current position?
- Is the drip tray large enough to hold enough water to thoroughly wet the entire growing medium?
- If there are no drainage holes, how quickly or slowly does the water evaporate or become absorbed by the plant? (See CONTAINERS for a simple checking method.)

Remember to water less often during the dormant or 'off' season, when the plant is not growing vigorously.

> *Hint: Water indoor plants with tepid or room-temperature water. Avoid excessive watering on foliage or crown of the plant (the point where all the foliage emerges). For sensitive plants, pour water in the drip tray rather than on the surface. Syringe foliage during the heat of the day if the foliage is susceptible to rapid drying out (some ferns and palms).*

The rewarding, easy to care for foliage of one of many Peperomia *varieties require medium light and moderate watering.*

Feeding indoor plants

Indoor plants need to be fed often, every 10–15 days during peak growing season. Feed less often when the plant is dormant, if this applies. It is a good idea is to feed with less fertiliser than recommended, but more often. Feed with foliage fertilisers for foliage plants and general balanced fertilisers for flowering plants. It is suggested that liquid organic foliar fertilisers are used where possible, as these fertilisers do not build up sugary deposits of chemicals on the surface or sides of containers and are very readily absorbed by the plants through the foliage or root systems. This means that less fertiliser is flushed through the drainage holes at the bottom of the pot. If chemical fertilisers are used, select a slow-release, granular fertiliser or a liquid fertiliser ideal for the type of plant or plants to be fed.

Growing medium

Many so-called 'potting soils' contain little or no soil at all. Loosely based on composted wood bark, peat, moisture-retaining components and drainage material such as silica sand, the mixtures vary from one source to another.

- A simple homemade general mixture could consist of:
  - □ one part well-rotted, sifted leaf compost,
  - □ one part swimming pool filter sand or similar, and
  - □ one part sterilised garden soil (to sterilise, spread 10–15 cm soil in a deep baking tray, in the oven, at 100°C for 30–45 minutes, remove and allow to cool).

- For acid-loving plants, the mixture should use acid leaves such as pine, cedar, and oak, *Erica* or *Protea* for compost.

- For more drainage add more sand.

- For plants preferring more moisture, add more compost.

- Mix all components together and add a moisture-retaining component – a chemical composition available from garden centres (crushed floral arranging blocks will help to a degree).

- Add fertiliser, if granular fertilisers are used: 30 g per large bucket of mix. If foliar fertilisers are to be used, wait until after planting, and apply as instructed on container.

Planting indoor plants

Cover the drainage holes with available synthetic felt products, squares of nylon socks or stockings, or a shallow layer of stone or broken pieces of pots. This is simply to prevent the growing medium from flushing through the holes when watering. It has no other function. Fill the container with the potting mixture, knock it down slightly, plant into the mixture and water well. The mixture may subside – top up with medium until plant and medium are level and just below the rim of the container. Do not allow the plant roots to stick out above the growing medium. Should this happen, remove the plant together with some growing medium and replant at the correct level. If the plant is being repotted, loosen the roots from the existing root ball and cut off some of the matted roots at the base of the root ball before replanting.

Pests and diseases

Diseases affecting indoor plants are similar to those that affect typical garden plants. In most cases, they are caused by similar conditions, too – waterlogged growing medium, poor ventilation, or high air and soil temperatures. To correct this, change position, growing medium and watering pattern. If the plant is diseased and the above points have been seen to, spray with systemic fungicides. In some cases it is best to destroy the plant and introduce a new one that is more tolerant of the conditions.

It is wise to consider the position of the plant and its sensitivity to particular pests. Hot, dry, poorly ventilated positions will encourage certain pests, while some plants are more susceptible to pests even when grown alongside other, less susceptible, plants in similar conditions. Rather buy the less susceptible plants for problem areas. See PESTS for general points.

INSECTS

Insects good and bad abound in every garden. Don't squash or spray everything that walks on more than four legs! It is important to know the difference between the insects that are beneficial and to be encouraged in the garden, and those that are not and need to be eradicated. If an environmental approach is favoured, most of what is sprayed in the garden acts as a deterrent, discouraging insects good and bad alike (unfortunately), but not necessarily killing them. If a more chemical approach is favoured, several pesticides have been developed that have a limited impact, usually targeted at specific insects or other pests, with little or no secondary poisoning. This means that birds, animals or other insects that feed on these dead insects or pests will not die. The range of more environmentally friendly and safe chemicals is increasing and regular visits to the pesticide shelves at the garden centres are essential, to keep up to date with current developments in this field. For the various methods of control, see PESTS.

It has been found that the healthier the garden, the less impact undesirable insects will have on it and the more the beneficial insects will breed. Yet another sound reason for regular feeding!

Insects should not only be regarded as creatures that do or don't eat plants, but as valuable contributors in other respects too, such as pollinators of some fruit trees, responsible for development of some seeds, a means of encouraging birds and other wildlife into the garden to feed, and adding a visual element to the garden simply by their presence – butterflies, bumble bees and dragonflies, for example.

INVADER PLANTS

Throughout South Africa's gardening history people have been introducing plants from elsewhere in the world. Many of these plants bypassed the proper channels of control and quarantine when they entered the country, 'escaped' from domestic gardens and have since become a threat to the environment. This, however, was not the only way in which invader plants arrived in South Africa. In some cases they were legally introduced, found the growing conditions to be better than those of their native country and began to multiply out of control. *Nerium oleander* in the Western Cape and the *Lantana camara* and black wattles in many warmer parts of the country are typical examples of the predicament.

These plants are mostly distributed by birds, animals, people and the weather, in the form of seed, although there are still people who propagate or dig up and transplant some invader weeds. There are numerous relevant publications and there are posters displayed in many plant outlets illustrating the plants that are listed as invaders. It is important that these plants are eradicated both in domestic gardens and in the wider environment. Remember that their removal is law and it is illegal to propagate, distribute or grow any of the listed alien invader plants.

IRRIGATION

There is a growing interest in domestic irrigation systems, which vary from very sophisticated to the most basic of layouts. The sophisticated sprinkler types can be gear rotated, moved by the impact of the water, opened and closed electronically, linked to various timing devices and even turned off in the event of rainy weather. Although nothing prevents the homeowner from installing these systems, it is recommended that they be at least designed by professionals.

For the enthusiastic DIY gardener there are more popular, simple, easy-to-install systems consisting of low-pressure networks with simple connections, low-cost replaceable spray nozzles, sprayers or micro-jets. The range available is extensive, with the simplest systems operating off a garden tap, with or without a manual or battery-operated timer installed between the pipes and the tap. When considering a system, check the following:

- What water pressure is available? This will have impact on the size of the area to be watered at any one time.

- Check the position of taps in relation to areas to be watered.

The well-known 'Pampas grass' is perhaps dramatic and attractive when the new plumes appear **but** *it's an invader weed and must be removed.*

- Does the area consist of lawn, planted areas or a mixture of both?
- What height are the plants to be watered, and can they be watered from above or below?
- With existing water pressure, how far apart will spray heads be spaced for ideal coverage?
- Do all areas of the garden require similar watering patterns, or can some areas be watered less and still survive?
- Identify areas where more water needs to be applied for specialised plantings.
- Decide how and where the main lines of the system will cross over existing hard surface areas and plan accordingly.

INSTALLATION

- Make sure that all components are selected for the specific system before beginning with installation.
- If the installation coincides with new planting areas, do not cover the pipelines until the plants have been planted, to avoid damaging main lines.
- If the system is laid on top of the soil, complete all soil shaping and planting first, then lay the main line where needed. This can be covered later with mulch or soil, where possible.
- If the system is to be covered, check all connections for leaks before covering the pipes.

- If a timer is incorporated, make sure that the area is watered well at the chosen time setting – adjust accordingly.
- To check coverage, place 4 or 5 equal-sized cups or tins at equal intervals (about a metre apart) in a line, from the spray head to the edge of the spray radius. Allow the water to spray for a period of time – 15 minutes, for example. Check the water level: it should be similar in all containers and 4–6 mm deep (providing roughly 25 mm water per hour, which is sufficient for most general garden situations). If the levels differ, the spray points are too close or too far apart, or incorrect nozzles are being used, or water pressure is too low to distribute water evenly over intended areas. If the level is less than 4–6 mm, too little water is being sprayed out over the area. Increase the watering time or the amount of water (by using fewer sprayers at one time). If there is more than 4–6 mm water, too much water is being sprayed; reduce the spraying time or increase the area to be sprayed (use more sprinklers at one time).
- Remember to reduce water volume and duration during the winter months; this applies particularly to warm season lawn types, deciduous plants and areas planted with winter annuals.
- Because of chemical build-up from municipal water in fine openings of some sprayers, it is important to clean them from time to time, or replace with new ones.

The better the irrigation layout is, the better the chance of a well-watered garden.

JACUZZI/SPA
PLANT PROBLEMS

There is a general trend in South Africa to install these types of baths indoors. Evaporation of heated water and water treatment chemicals within the same enclosed space creates humid, chemically saturated, warm conditions, which are generally ideal for the user, but almost totally unsuitable for the plants used to enhance these areas. Few plants survive for any period of time, and although some jacuzzi designs include plant spaces these should be seen as areas to display plants for short periods of time rather than permanent plant display areas. Rather leave the plants in their original containers and place them in the planting areas with bark or other covering to conceal their containers.

Flowering indoor plants will have a very limited lifespan. Foliage plants will survive longer, and of these *Ficus*, *Schefflera*, *Aglaonema* and *Aralia* will last longest. Ferns, palms, *Philodendron* and 'delicious monster' are least successful. If possible, remove the plants from time to time and care for them under more favourable conditions. An alternative is to make use of 'silk' plants with live, flowering plants as short-term fillers.

If there is uncertainty regarding plants' survival near a jacuzzi, don't plant them in the 'garden areas' provided, but keep them in their containers and move them around from time to time.

KIDDIES' GARDENS

Kids love a challenge, and there is a lot of fun and challenge to be had from owning their own garden in which to sow seed and grow plants, whether these are herbs, flowers or vegetables.

- Keep the area small and easy to maintain.
- Surround it with some form of permanent edge, such as logs, stones, bricks or plastic bed edging.
- Make it interesting, incorporate a bench, swing, and a Wendy-house or play area.
- Keep it bright and sunny, with lots of colour.
- Encourage the kids to personally work in the garden.
- Allow them to select their own seedlings or packets of seed. (Check the back of the packets to see how long the seeds will take to germinate. Nothing discourages a young gardener more than plants that take too long to 'do' anything.)
- There are kiddie-sized garden tools, which help them feel it's all their own space.

- Explain why things are done in a garden; feeding, weeding, watering, and so on.
- Keep the interest going by joining a kiddie garden club at the local garden centre; buy literature, show interest – use the vegetables and help pick the flowers!

Some ideal kiddie plants to consider
Sunflower, marigold, balsam, nasturtium, *Cosmos*, sweet peas, radish, bush beans, peas, lettuce, tomato, various aromatic and tasty herbs, miniature rose bushes, strawberries, spring bulbs, *Amaryllis*, low-growing *Dahlias* and *Liliums* or scented shrubs.

Simply by adding the appropriate ornaments, kids can be encouraged to garden.

Sunflowers are quick and easy plants to grow from seed in the kiddies' garden.

KITCHEN GARDENS

A kitchen garden was traditionally an area where vegetables, cut flowers and herbs were grown for domestic use, often adjacent to the kitchen area of the home. The general trend today is to use such an area for containers, water features and small interesting areas of garden space, and the remainder is paved. The retractable wash line facilities, 'al fresco' tables and chairs, raised planting areas and potting/seed sowing areas have also become popular aspects of these gardens. In years past kitchen gardens were large and functional; nowadays they are smaller, more intimate and interesting. Quick crop, novel vegetables can be grown among herbs and cut flower annuals. Surfaces are simple, rustic and practical.

Because of the heat given off by walls and paving it is wise to mulch the area heavily, make sure pots do not dry out and consider an umbrella for instant, temporary shade. Moving water will help to add a cooling sound effect. These areas are often ideal for tender plants that will not grow in the more exposed parts of the garden. Should space allow, the kitchen garden is an ideal area to raise seedlings, establish alternative pots of colour for use elsewhere in the garden or make compost in a series of compost bins. The ideal is to make the area functional, and at the same time, interesting.

A well-planned kitchen garden provides space colour, herbs, vegetables and maybe even a work area.

LAYERING

Layering is a simple, easy means of propagating young plants from an existing plant in the garden. Although it will not be successful in all cases, there are sufficient popular plants that can be layered to justify giving it a mention.

The process is a simple one. In the case of shrubs, soft willowy growth is stripped of the lower two-thirds of its foliage, bent down from the main plant and pegged to the ground with a wire stay. Cover the stem pegged to the ground with soil. Growth from creepers can be pulled down and pegged in the same way. Most creepers can be grown in this manner, allowing numerous plants to be propagated from limited resources.

Any bud in the middle, stripped, section of the branch, which comes in contact with the soil can be given a slight nick just below the bud (traditionally, this nick was held open by a small piece of charcoal or toothpick), before it is held firmly against the soil. The end of the branch protrudes beyond the pegged soil-covered area. In time, the nicked area will develop roots, and once these roots are firmly established, the plant can be severed from the main plant, removed, and planted out elsewhere. This can be done with several branches at the same time, each radiating out from the main plant.

Some of the shrubs that can be propagated in this manner: most creeper and bush jasmine, *Magnolia purpurea*, berry fruits such as blackberries, some low-growing juniper varieties, *Cotoneaster*, *Hydrangea*, honeysuckle, willow, elderberry, *Wisteria*, *Viburnum*, *Plumbago*, *Tecoma* (*Tecomaria*), ivy varieties, *Banksia*, holly and *Euonymus* species.

A more complicated form of layering can be practised with some plants. These plants are cut off at ground level and mounded with soil. As the new growth emerges it roots in the mound of soil. Once rooting is well established, the rooted plants can be severed from the main plant. This form of layering is ideal for *Hydrangea*, May bushes (*Spiraea*), and *Chrysanthemums*.

Yet another form of layering, known as air layering, is used to produce plants from plant material that has become woody and bare of leaves. This is ideal for propagating from leggy indoors foliage plants such as *Ficus*, *Schefflera* or *Dracaena*. The process includes cutting slight nicks in the stem of the plant below one or two dormant buds, wrapping wet moss firmly around the nicked areas and sealing this entire section of the stem tightly in plastic. This in turn, can be sealed with tree sealer, or electrical tape – it must be airtight. With time, roots will develop within the moss ball. Once signs of renewed growth and vigour are apparent above this rooted area, the plant can be cut from the main plant and potted up to develop further.

LIGHTING IN THE GARDEN

Often considered too expensive and complicated to install, garden lighting has made slow progress in the domestic garden, but it offers several options:

- General lighting to brightly illuminate an area.
- Selected lighting to illuminate specific areas, pathways or entrances.
- Design lighting installed to enhance aspects of the garden – water features, specific plantings or select

Select lighting in a garden can add an entire new atmosphere to it.

garden features. These are often designed to be part of the garden as seen from a particular viewpoint, such as patio or poolside.

Lighting can be installed to provide various effects:

- Security lights – for obvious reasons.
- Spotlights – focused on a specific area.
- Floodlights – for general illumination.
- Down lights – to illuminate footpaths, driveways, entrances or steps.
- Up lights – used in plantings or near structures to illuminate from below.
- Decorative lights – to accentuate a specific fantasy in the garden.

Although installation is not regarded as a domestic do-it-yourself task, it is wise to identify the type of effect needed before calling in an expert. Consider the type of light fittings needed and how they will add to and accentuate the specific design of the garden or home. Should they stand tall in the garden, obvious and in a style typical of the garden? Perhaps they need to be hidden away, weatherproofed and inconspicuous.

OTHER CONSIDERATIONS

- Some light fittings are installed as part of structures, walls or steps, and forward planning is essential to ensure the correct position and effect.
- Will the various lights work on time switches or be activated manually?
- Where will the power come from, and where will cables be laid?
- Consider maintenance of the installations, once installed.
- Make sure the fittings are durable, resistant to weather and practical, with replaceable working parts, such as bulbs, sockets, switches, etc.
- Consider low-voltage lighting for added safety.
- Garden lighting can add a new dimension to gardens after dark, even if installation is limited to a selected area of the garden.
- Remember, it is wise to employ an expert to install these lights – electricity, water and weather make poor bedfellows.

LITERATURE

Much of the available garden literature was written in the northern hemisphere. This means that there must be a reversal of seasons and relevant months when related to gardening in the southern hemisphere. When selecting books look at the following:

Books on general gardening – good local books are a first option. (Unfortunately there is still a limited range available, but more indigenous plant books are being published of late.)

Second option – overseas books that are not too hemisphere specific, providing general information rather than information on plant material only suitable for their area.

Third option – books on specific plant types, with growing requirements, which are universal.

Final option – specialised reference books, with plant-specific information, relevant to growing requirements, species and varieties available. Either published in the form of encyclopaedias or botanical works on a specific genus. If local plant catalogues are available, these make an ideal reference to plants locally available, their current local names and performance in their areas of availability.

Books on landscape design are considerably more international, as design concepts stay the same, although the plants suggested may change. Well-illustrated books and magazines often help formulate an idea, although the plants illustrated may not be locally available. Buy or refer to books that use colour photos rather than hand-drawn illustrations. Photos provide an element of accuracy, whereas hand-drawn illustrations often do not, unless they are detailed botanical drawings.

As new plants are developed it is important to continue to gather books to ensure that new, relevant information can be accessed. It is important to remember that plant names change: should the book collection be dated, it may be difficult to trace plants, their new names, and their relevant information. Avoid, cheap 'no-real-information' books. Once paged through, these books will seldom be referred to again.

MANURE

This is a general term given to organic waste of animals (and in some countries, that of humans too). Processed human waste, available from some water purification plants, is in most cases purchased on contract and used in bulk for agricultural purposes. The more typical manures available for domestic garden situations are chicken litter, kraal manure and horse manure. All three of these are extremely strong when fresh, and can damage or kill off plant material. Smaller quantities of sheep, rabbit or pig manure are available in some areas, but are not commonly considered unless the source and supply are regular.

For best effects, all types of manure should be old, well rotted and used carefully. If there is any hint of ammonia when spreading the manure it is still too fresh. If manures are used in conjunction with compost, apply rock phosphates (a natural form of phosphates) or bone meal, as their decomposition is enhanced when used in conjunction with manures and their effectiveness is more apparent, in terms of plant performance and health.

If used when planting new plants, mix the manure (no more than one third of the soil volume) well into the soil, rather than leaving a layer that could damage new roots as they develop and grow into it.

> *Hint: Manure soaked in water – a plastic potato or orange pocket half filled, soaked for a week in a 44-gallon drum of water – will make an ideal liquid fertiliser for vegetables and flowering plants.*
>
> *Diluted one to one with water, the solution can serve as a mild liquid feed for new seedlings and containerised plants.*

If a source of pig or sheep manure is available, do not use too much too often, as there are metal deposits in these manures which are not too beneficial to plants if used in large quantities, too regularly. Chicken litter is an ideal compost activator if spread dry among the composted material. As long as the litter is dry and old, there is no specific quantity limit.

If manure is to be used as a mulch, it would need to be spread 3–5 cm thick, two or three times during a growing season. Little or no value is gained from spreading manure as mulch during the dormant period.

MOLES

Perhaps one of the most annoying creatures to invade any garden is a mole or mole-rat. Golden moles are reasonably harmless insectivorous animals that burrow just under the surface in search of grubs, earthworms and other burrowing insects. Should they chew through roots, it is generally to get where they are going. Moles appear to be more active in the coastal regions, and their telltale signs are soft, hollow ridges (and molehills thrown up from the deeper diggings) visible on the surface of the lawn or flowerbeds.

Mole-rats, on the other hand, are herbivorous and can burrow deep into the soil in search of the right root, tuber, bulb or corm. They can easily denude a garden of all edible roots in a short space of time. Like all other rodents, they are prolific breeders and can comfortably make any garden their own, pushing up soil mounds as they burrow in various directions. Mole-rats are active almost throughout the country, and contrary to a popular belief they are not a protected species. (The Golden moles are, though.)

Control of these pests is as much urban legend as reality. Numerous 'foolproof' mole-rat killing or mole chasing methods exist, all said to 'work every time' by the narrator, only proving to be yet another disappointment in the end. It must be remembered that moles (as a collective title) have acute hearing and sense of smell. They can hear when people approach and begin opening up the hole or tunnel, and they can smell if anything dropped into the hole has been handled by humans. It is important to tread softly when approaching the mole-heap. Wear gloves or two plastic bags when preparing any bait, handle it as little as possible and use tongs to carry it to the hole.

Methods of control fall into three sections – but it must be said that there is no guarantee that any method will be constantly effective.

Chemical methods consist mainly of various tablets, all of which break down when in contact with the moist soil, giving off poisonous gases that kill the moles. There is a more friendly commercially available method, based on a concentrated garlic extract; this chases the moles away rather than killing them.

Mechanical gadgets are inserted in the tunnels and either catch the mole alive in a tube-like apparatus or are spring-loaded pincers, which squeeze the mole to death.

Environmental methods, as opposed to mythical methods, are numerous:

- Some plants, when grown in the garden, will deter mole activity. They vary from area to area, but most of them seem to be plants that aromatically impregnate the soil in which they are grown, such as garlic, garlic chives, *Tulbaghia*, various *Alocasia* (known in KwaZulu-Natal as 'madumbi') and *Euphorbia* species.

- Close-woven wire-mesh baskets set into the soil in which bulbs may be grown.

- Dog litter pushed into the tunnels (I have my doubts about this one).

Numerous soil mounds in the lawn and eaten-off, dying plants are often the only indications of a mole in the garden.

- Thorny branches buried among or around bulbs and other edible plants.

- Recently, a piece of equipment that emits a high-pitched sound has become available. This is placed on or in the ground and the sound repels the moles! (I have my doubts about this one too.)

MOON CHARTS

This is a gardening principle from as far back as the twelfth century, and it still has a strong following today amongst some gardeners.

There are said to be eight phases of the moon, and followers of moon planting techniques divide gardening activities into each of these phases.

- New moon is a time to plant.

- Waxing crescent is a time to thin out seedlings.

- First quarter is a time to feed.

- Waxing gibbous or convex phase is when plants draw most nutrients from the soil.

- Full moon is time to harvest.

- Waning gibbous or convex phase is when ripening occurs.

- Last quarter is time to recycle or make compost.

- Waning crescent is a time to make ready for the new cycle.

Circular charts are designed to be used in conjunction with the days of the month and the moon phases to calculate when to sow, plant and harvest crops and prepare the soil. These charts are available from specialist suppliers and usually come with instructions on how to set them up and interpret the information. Limited literature is published, and interested gardeners will have to hunt for sufficient information regarding this interesting and ancient gardening method.

MOVING PLANTS

Certain plants can be moved from one place to another, if factors necessary for success are considered:

- Plants that have been growing in a specific position for a considerable length of time may need to be cut back severely before they can be moved. All plants that are moved should be cut back by roughly one third of growth, to compensate for root loss during moving.

- Deciduous plants should be moved in winter, when they have dropped their leaves. In this case cutting back is not necessary unless the plant is too large and has stood for a considerable time in its current position.

- Evergreen plants should be moved just before the emergence of their new foliage in late winter/early spring. Alternatively, move once the new growth has matured in midsummer.

- If possible, long-term root preparation will mean a greater level of success when moving the plant (see below).

> **Hint:** *It is important to mark north on a plant before moving it, particularly if it has grown in one position for more than 18 months. The plant can be marked with a dab of paint, a piece of coloured yarn or a removable plant tag.*

Most Australian and Western Cape (fynbos) plant material does not move successfully. This includes *Proteas*, *Ericas* and *Leucospermums* (pincushions) from the Western Cape as well as *Grevilleas*, *Melaleuca*, *Pittosporum*, *Banksias* and *Eucalyptus* from Australia.

Plants that have matured in size are difficult to move without professional help, as the size of the root ball they need to re-grow is too heavy to move manually.

It is unwise to reduce the root ball to a manageable size. The root ball extent is determined by the size of the plant to be moved, and is directly responsible for the transplant success.

How to move plants

- Identify north on the plant to be moved.

- Cut back the plant, if the shape allows (not shapes like *Aloes* or cycads) and if it's necessary.

- Prepare the hole in the new position and make sure that it is large enough to manoeuvre the plant in.

- Dig a trench 50 cm away from the base of the plant, 30–50 cm deep and the width of a spade. Dig this trench right round the plant, leaving a root ball that is still attached through its base.

- Firmly wrap the round root ball in hessian – this will be planted with the plant.

- If time allows, refill the trench with peat moss or sawdust and allow 6–8 weeks for new roots to develop.

- If time does not allow, spray the plant with an anti-transpirant such as 'Wiltpruf', no more than 5 hours before moving; after this cut through the base of the root ball.

- Fill the new hole with water and allow this to soak away.

- Move the plant to the new site and realign with north.

- Place the root ball in the hole and make sure the root ball soil is level with the surrounding soil level.

- Fill the surrounding space in the hole with a mixture of equal parts compost and soil.

- If the plant needs to be staked, insert at least two stakes firmly on either side of the root ball.

- Water well, and as the soil subsides add more soil until the root ball is firmly set in soil. Any remaining soil can be used as a low dam wall around the newly planted shrub/ tree. This wall can be levelled off as the plant becomes established.

- Water thoroughly once or twice a week, allowing the water to soak away *completely* in between waterings.

MULCH

Anything that covers the exposed ground between plants can be called a 'mulch'. Mulch serves several common yet simple purposes:

- Mulching exposed garden surfaces prevents evaporation.

- It helps soil from becoming compacted by rain or watering.

- Covering the soil with organic mulch reduces the chances of weed (or any seed) germination.

- It makes it difficult for garden pests, particularly snails and slugs, to move from area to area.

LEFT: Gravel is the perfect solution for service areas and casual pathways, keeping the area tidy and moist.

RIGHT: Seedpods can be used as an attractive mulch whilst they break down and add nutrients to the soil. Here the large seedpods of an Acacia sp. add texture to a small area in a garden.

- Mulching sloped surfaces reduces erosion.
- Well-mulched soil conserves water, which means watering occurs less often, and the evaporation rate is reduced.
- Non-compacted, moist soil encourages root development and healthy plant growth.

There is no limit to what can be used as mulch. Availability is often the deciding factor. Mulch can be divided into two basic types.

Inorganic mulches
Gravel, pebbles, paving slabs, stepping stones, random pieces of slate or stone and to a lesser degree sand, will all serve as a mulch if used between plants, on open soil areas or as semi-hard surfaces between groundcovers or annuals. Close-woven plastic sheeting, or in some cases solid black plastic sheeting, is used as a form of mulch reducing weed growth, retaining moisture and keeping crops clean – strawberries for example are planted in beds covered in this way, with holes cut for the plants to grow through.

More important than what is used, is how thick a layer is used. Solid slabs need to be placed reasonably close together – 10 cm apart, with either plants, pebbles or gravel in between. Loose inorganic mulch material such as gravel, pebbles, crushed brick, etc. should be at least 7,5 cm thick or thicker. Sand tends to allow for evaporation and seed germination; as a result is it more successful if used in conjunction with other materials such as closely woven plastic sheeting.

Organic mulches
Leaves, lawn clippings, rough compost, straw, cut veld grass, bark nuggets, nutshells, wood chips, and in some cases shredded paper or cardboard are used. It must be remembered that almost all of these have a limited lifespan, and will need to be replaced from time to time. In most cases 7,5 cm thick layers are the minimum, but there is no limit to how much is used; again, availability is often the determining factor.

Where fresh organics such as leaves, wood chips and lawn clippings are used, extra nitrogen will have to be added to the soil (30 g LAN per square metre will suffice) if these organics are dug into the soil at any stage. The reason for this is that they draw nitrogen from the soil to assist in decomposition (denitrification). This often results in the growth of plants being pale green or yellowed.

The organics are often dug into the soil as new material is made available, such as leaves falling in autumn, or lawn clippings being cut during summer. In both cases, the new material can be laid down in layers during the season, and used as mulch until the beginning of the new season.

If compost is used as mulch, make sure that it is not too fine. Keep the rough un-decomposed material and spread as a mulch direct from the heap. (If it is too fine, seeds will germinate, and it will compact, like soil, with watering and rain.)

If mulching and fertilising take place at the same time, apply the fertiliser first and then mulch on top of this. If moisture-retaining products are used, these are dug into the soil before spreading the mulch. If commercial mulch is purchased, one bag should cover approximately 1–1,5 square metres. Make sure that the mulch is in contact with the soil, not lying on plant material and not too loosely packed.

Mulch with autumn leaves to protect the base of the more tender plants – used here to protect purple flowering Heliotrope.

NEW PLANTS IN THE GARDEN

Buying new plants is a simple task, but there are points that need to be considered if they are to make a worthwhile addition to the garden. Failing to do so often results in a plant contributing very little – in fact, it often appears to have been 'squeezed in'. There is also the chance that if all growing requirements are not considered the new plant may not survive to reach maturity.

Points to consider

- What size space is available? Knowing this makes it possible to buy the correct plant for the space.

- What plants are growing nearby? Considering this allows a new plant to visually become a part of an existing planting. Otherwise new plants can appear to be 'added on'.

- What are the specific growing conditions of the area where the new plants are to be planted? Aspects such as soil type, sun/shade and water requirements ensure correct selection and better performance of plants.

- Are the new plants expected to play a specific role in the garden, whether decorative (adding to a current theme, emphasising an existing feature, etc.), or functional (screening off an area, creating a windbreak or hiding an ugly view)? Decide which and select plants accordingly.

- Consider the seasonal weather changes and effects – some plants can withstand low temperatures in winter, but other plants can be affected by cold, particularly when newly planted and young. Don't plant tender plants unless there are protected areas in which to plant them.

Novel aspects of a plant can often result in it being introduced as a new plant, such as the variegated leaves of this nasturtium.

- Look for healthy, well-grown plants – these will have the best chances of survival and success.

- Slightly tender plants should only be planted when all fear of frost is past, yet early enough to establish themselves before the following winter.

- Don't buy plants grown and sold in different climatic areas – e.g. from the Cape to inland or coastal areas; especially not from overseas – because acclimatisation in another area could be a long and often unsuccessful process.

Adding new plants to an existing garden space may have its problems:

- Root competition from other established plants could limit growing space for the new plants, thus restricting growth.

- Compacted soil conditions could inhibit root development, unless a well-prepared hole is dug.

- Established plants tend to absorb more water than newly planted ones, which can result in the new plant drying out – water often until new plants are established.

- Established plants have specific shadow patterns; make sure these do not adversely influence new plants.

To plant new plants

- Make sure the area is well prepared: a hole at least twice the size of the bag is advisable. A square hole will prevent the roots from growing round in circles before penetrating into the surrounding soil area.

- Make sure the plant is planted level with surrounding soil level. Remove the plastic bag or pot and the plant label. If a stake supports the plant, attach the plant label to this, so that it is still visible but does not inhibit plant growth. A plastic plant label can strangle the stem of a growing plant.

- If the soil removed from the hole is of poor quality, replace it with soil imported from elsewhere. Replace one third of the soil with compost or well-rotted kraal manure. Appropriate fertilisers should be added (see FERTILISERS).

- Tramp the soil down firmly once the plant has been planted.

- Because the soil mixture into which the plants are placed probably contains fertilisers, the next feeding application need only be six weeks after planting. If the plant is planted during winter, do not feed again after planting, until the beginning of the new growing season (late August).

- If the new plants grow vigorously in the first season it is an idea to cut them back by one third at the end of the first growing season. This encourages the plants to bush out more and not readily develop bare stems near the base as they mature. (This applies to almost all plants except special form plants such as *Aloes*, palms and cycads.)

NUTRIENTS

Nutrients are the chemicals in the soil that keep plants alive, healthy and growing properly. They help a plant ward off disease, bear flowers, and produce healthy seed and or fruit. The nutrients that plants require are not only or essentially provided by fertilisers. All forms of plant-usable organics will provide nutrients; it is simply a question of how beneficial the nutrients will be. In some cases, organic material will improve the texture of the soil, but won't add any nutritional value.

Compost

A very loose term for organic material that has been decomposed in heaps, pits or bins. Depending on the material used, heat generated and moisture content of material during the decomposition process and time frame, this material can add nutritional value to the soil. It may, in cases where the material is too dry, or left too long before use, play more of a moisture-conserving and drainage-enhancing role in the soil than a nutritional one.

Manure

Manure of various origins is available, varying from farm animal and human waste to bat and seabird guano. Used in small quantities, with regular applications, most of these will provide readily absorbed nutrients. Some manures are strong when fresh and can damage plant foliage or roots. These must be left to age or be used in small quantities, sparsely applied and watered well into the soil. The droppings of most domestic pets have no nutritional value and are best added to the compost heap or discarded.

For a constantly healthy appearance, plants in containers must be fed regularly, preferably with a foliar feeding.

To get the best effect with short-lived annuals or other flowering plants, regular feeding is essential.

Leaf mould

A term given to composted heaps of gathered leaves. Some leaves, generally the soft deciduous leaves, when decomposed are high in nutrition whilst others, the harder, leathery, often evergreen leaves, add little or no nutritional value to the soil. The more leathery, hard and slow to decompose leaves such as *Eucalyptus*, plane tree, loquat or evergreen oak are best added to compost heaps or burnt to provide limited quantities of potash. Some leaves, e.g. birch, appear to add enzymes to the soil that inhibit the growth of other plants, while some, e.g. oak and pine, provide plant nutrients but at the same time make the pH of the soil acid.

Green manure

A practice less popular today but still used in small-scale agriculture where feasible. Nitrogen-fixing plants such as beans, soya beans or lucerne are allowed to grow until semi-matured, then ploughed back into the soil and allowed to decompose before sowing other nitrogen-demanding plants in the same area. Generally, in a garden situation, it is not regarded as practical; however, lucerne, lupins or oats can be planted and dug back into the soil when 20 cm tall. This practice can be applied to proposed vegetable areas or areas where new shrubberies are proposed at a later stage. The nutritional value is generally short-lived, but the quality of the soil is greatly improved by doing this.

Natural chemicals

Certain basic chemicals can be used to provide plants with specific nutrients. This implies that other means must be employed to ensure a balanced nutritional programme.

- Rock phosphates – will slowly decompose and add phosphates to the soil. This is particularly effective if used in conjunction with well-rotted kraal manure.

- Agricultural or dolomitic lime – will help break down 'brak' soil conditions.

'Brak' soil is a soil condition usually associated with high levels of harmful sodium salts that are water-soluble, such as common salt. Drainage is usually very poor and there is an undesirably high percentage of clay in the soil profile. Lime will also slowly change the pH of the soil and repeated applications can result in yellow growth on some acid-loving plants.

- Flowers of sulphur is a perfect natural fungicide, which can be added to plants when they are being moved, split up or transplanted. It can also be added to plants that enjoy acid conditions. Add only in the growing season, using small quantities (30 g per square metre) and apply once a year. Sulphur is slow to break down in the soil but the higher summer soil temperatures will help.

- Epsom salts, magnesium sulphate and alum are sometimes used, but they may have less real effect on plants than balanced fertilisers.

- If single chemicals are to be used it is important that a thorough knowledge of this form of plant feeding is acquired first. A comprehensive book on hydroponics could help.

Formulated chemicals

Specific formulated chemical fertilisers are designed to feed a specific range of plants in a specific way, for a regulated time span or for a specific purpose. Some of these fertilisers will provide balanced nutrients for a special range of plants – for example, *Hydrangea* concentrate, orchid fertiliser, fertiliser for acid-loving plants, cacti, annuals, foliage or flowering container plants.

Though best used for the correct plants, there will be little or no adverse effects if used on plants in general.

To keep good colour – either pink or blue – Hydrangeas *have to be given the correct feeding.*

ORGANIC GARDENING

Simply, this is a method of gardening where all aspects of soil care, plant nutrition, pest and disease control and general garden care are based on sound organic methods. No manufactured chemical products are used where an organic alternative is available. Vast strides have been made in organic gardening awareness, and organic fruit and vegetable as well as general organic farming are becoming common. Despite its growing popularity, there is still a tendency to interpret this approach to gardening as slow and fussy, but this is not the case. The methods used are more thorough and time consuming, but the end result is decidedly worth considering.

Permaculture is an advanced development in this method of gardening. This is a comprehensive organic growing method, usually applied to food crops, which ensures, by planting selected plants together, that the overall health of the soil and the plants' wellbeing are maintained, whilst producing healthy crops. The selection of plants is often multi-levelled,

creating specific environments for the various plants grouped together. The plant selection would include legumes such as beans or sweet peas to enrich the soil and pungent plants such as marigolds, garlic or *Tulbachia* as insect repellent plants.

Take care, when gardening with organics, to ensure that the plant nutrients are balanced, provided as needed and in quantities that will benefit the plant material – difficult to gauge with this system of gardening, as the products used are not always in measurable quantities. Although this gardening method is regarded, and rightly so, as the more natural form of plant and soil care, there are no 'quick fix' methods, and building up soil quality is often a slow and demanding process. It must be realised that the concept of organic gardening is a natural one designed to counteract the more common, quick, chemical approach and it is important to remember that the plants must not be disadvantaged in any way simply because the organic route has been chosen. A good working knowledge of the nutrient value of the organics used will be necessary to ensure that the plants receive balanced feeding.

In the case of pest and disease control, short-term deterrent treat-ments tend

to be applied rather than chemical 'kill' tactics. Many treatments are based on plant extracts, aromas and oils, and as watering or rain can wash many of these preparations off, regular applications need to be applied. (See also ENVIRONMENTAL CONTROL.)

Before venturing into an all-organic approach, refer to reliable books and consider becoming a member of a local organic soil association.

ORNAMENTAL GRASSES

Unlike lawn grasses, ornamental grasses are plants whose role in the garden depends on their size, colour, shape or seasonal changes. Although most of them are clump-forming plants, there are some that will spread. This includes many bamboo species, *Phalaris* (gardener's garters) and *Arundo donax variegata* (tall ribbon grass). These should be used in large areas or in positions where their spreading will not have an adverse impact on other nearby plants. To contain them, an edging (galvanised metal sheeting works well) can be embedded into the ground at least

The low-growing fine foliage of Holcus mollis variegatus *contrasts well with taller variegated grasses.*

30–50 cm deep (and allow for overlapping) to completely surround the desired area. An alternative for smaller spreading species is to plant into a buried plastic container or drum with the bottom cut out of it. Many of the spreading plants, particularly bamboo, only send out new runners at the beginning of the growing season – September/October. Shoots that appear in unwanted positions can simply be snapped off at ground level and that runner will grow no further.

Some, not many, ornamental grasses are annual: 'bunny tail' (*Lagurus ovata*), and 'quaking' grass (*Briza maxima* and *B. minima*), are popular species. These are usually grown for their seed heads, which mature quickly and dry well, and are often purchased dried and dyed various colours. The perennial species contribute points of interest in a garden. Many of them are evergreen and in some cases totally unaffected by cold. Though not true grasses, the Cape 'thatch grasses' such as *Elegia capensis* and *Chondropetalum tectorum* are two such valuable grass-like forms. They can enhance any theme, from an oriental to a dune-like effect, or simply be used as a dramatic focus in a general planting.

Many of the ornamental grasses originate in Europe and are deciduous or react to frost, changing colour as the weather gets colder. It is not necessary to cut them down as soon as they are frosted; rather enjoy the change in colour and cut them back in early spring as new growth begins to appear.

Once ornamental grasses begin to develop there is little to do to maintain them other than regular feeding and seasonal cutting back of untidy old growth. This must be timed to not damage the new growth. Generally an ideal time is at the end of the growing season, after the frosts and before the new season. This provides the best of both seasons – the new growth and the winter colour. For evergreen grasses, any time during the growing season is ideal for cutting back and splitting up the clumps. Feed generously at the beginning of the growing season with 60 g balanced fertiliser per plant or square metre.

A large number of the ornamental grasses do not set reliable seed and can only be increased by dividing existing plants. This also applies to other plants, which, although not true grasses, are grass-like and can be used and treated similarly. Many of these 'grasses' belong to the lily family and bear spikes of small blue, white, or mauve flowers, and blue or black seeds. These plants – such as *Ophiopogon* species (Mondo grass) or *Liriope* species (tuft lilies) – are ideal groundcovers or specimen plants among pebbles and near ponds; the very dwarf Mondo grass *Ophiopogon japonicus* 'Kyoto dwarf' is an ideal plant to use among stepping stones and rocks.

Bold-leafed bamboo-like ornamental grass, needs to be cut back from time to time to keep it tidy. It can be tender in cold winters.

PAINT IN THE GARDEN

With climatic contrasts as severe as they are in South Africa, most wood and iron outdoor equipment and accessories weather quickly. Without timely maintenance, unnecessary losses can be the end result. Paint, if chosen correctly and applied properly, goes a long way to preserving the life of almost all perishable outdoor items. Not only does it have a preserving function, but the vast range of colours and combinations of colour available breathe new life into many weather-beaten or boring outdoor items.

The range of paint types available ensures that anything that can be painted, and a few other items besides, can be smartened up with a paint formulated for its specific application. Metal and wood objects should be correctly primed and painted with oil-based (enamel) paints. It is important to make sure that the item has been properly cleaned and prepared first. Care must be taken to remove all rust or rotting wood and sand off any old paint to a manageable surface.

Wood structures could be treated with wood-preserving products or varnishes as an alternative to paints. Remember that some wood stains are not wood-preserving agents, merely colouring products. Asbestos-cement, concrete or plastered structures or objects should be scrubbed clean and dust free and given at least two coats of a good-quality outdoor acrylic (water-based) paint.

Always consult a paint specialist when considering any paint projects. Buy good quality paint and apply it properly with the correct equipment, in the ideal weather conditions.

Well-cared for garden furniture adds a sense of 'crisp newness' to a garden.

PALMS, CYCADS AND BAMBOO

Although these plants can be cared for as easily as any other garden or indoor plants, there is a strange perception that they are 'tricky' or problematic.

PALMS are popular both as garden and indoor plants. Indoor palms tend to be those that cannot grow outdoors in all parts of the country. In the warmer parts of the country, where severe cold and frost are not a factor, all palms generally available can be grown outdoors.

Many palms grow well in containers, but guard against growing the large, vigorous species in containers as their roots tend to break out of even the sturdiest of containers in a reasonably short space of time – *Phoenix canariensis* and *P. reticulata* are good examples. Avoid planting large palm species too near paving, garden walls and ponds or swimming pools – although their roots are strictly speaking not destructive, there are a lot of them as the palms begin to mature. Most smaller and slow-growing palm species and varieties will be able to grow in the same container for quite a long period, in fact some palms rather enjoy being root-bound.

Although palms are often associated with the sea and windswept beaches, they generally prefer well-drained growing conditions combined with regular watering. Some palms, such as some fish-tail palms (*Caryota* species), die after they have flowered and produced seed, so in areas where they can be grown it is a good idea to plant young ones every few years where needed.

Most palm fronds will live for a number of years before they die off. It is not essential that these are removed manually, as they will fall off in time; the physical cutting off of old fronds and tidying up the stem is more for aesthetics' sake than anything else. Although planting other plants inside old palm frond stumps can look nice,

Palms add a tropical graciousness to a garden and some palms will do this even in quite cold areas.

A cluster of ripe Phoenix reclinata *seed provides a burst of colour from time to time – and feeds some birds too.*

I suspect that it might invite unwanted nesting birds and rodents.

Outdoor palms have few diseases or pests, although I have seen a borer or beetle that ate out the heart of several palms in Durban, causing the crown to die off slowly. Palms grown indoors are often infested with woolly aphids, mealy bug and scale – perhaps due to poor air circulation, lack of general cleaning, poor watering programme and generally inconsistent attention to their wellbeing. They also suffer from brown edges on the fronds, fronds dying off too soon, and in the case of golden bamboo palms (*Chrysalidocarpus lutescens*), young side shoots dying off. Rethink the watering programme, light quality and winter room temperatures – one or all of these are not palm health friendly! All palms respond to regular feeding and water, particularly when young and newly planted.

CYCADS – a common name given to both the indigenous varieties (*Encephalartos* and *Stangeria* species) and the exotic species such as *Cycas*, *Zamia*, *Macrozamia*, and others less popular but collected by enthusiasts. Do not buy illegally collected cycads from dubious sources: many of them are fitted with tracking devices and all of them will have been stolen. In the case of all indigenous cycads you need to keep the receipt (in the case of young seedlings) or obtain a permit to own a cycad. No permit is needed for exotic varieties. All parts of the indigenous species should be regarded as toxic, despite the common name of 'broodboom' or 'bread tree'.

All cycads will grow well in containers, as long as they are well watered and fed, but none make good long-term indoor plants. The popular conception that they need not be fed is wrong (see FERTILISERS). Generally cycads are little affected by pests and diseases, but there are caterpillars that if allowed to hatch and develop will readily devour an entire new leaf crop in a short space of time.

Some of the indigenous 'cycads' are frost tender as well as being susceptible to sunburn. Specialised literature and experts will help you in selecting the right varieties for the right position. I have found that the species with blue-green foliage, such as *E. horridus*, *E. lehmannii* and *E. lanatus*, are an ideal choice for open, sunny, exposed areas. Generally the greener and shinier the foliage, the more they prefer shade and are frost sensitive. *Cycas revoluta* (sago palm) is decidedly the easiest of exotic cycads to grow, with little or no problems, hardy, tolerant of both sun and semi-shade and reasonably quick growing. It can be propagated from the side suckers it produces with age, or, if available, from seed.

Most cycads will transplant readily if most of the fronds are removed, the plant is reorientated to north, they are not over-watered, their roots are dusted thoroughly with a fungicide such as flowers of sulphur, and they are left, unfed, until new fronds appear – this can, in some cases, take a few years. Only remove foliage when transplanting well-established plants (see MOVING PLANTS) or when they begin to sag and die off. The leaf fronds have a reasonably long life and mature plants with more than one year's growth have a fuller, more dramatic effect.

BAMBOO is perhaps the most dramatic of the grass family, serving not only as a dramatic garden plant but also as a food source and a building material. There is some confusion as to its behaviour: it is perceived to be aggressively invasive, unsuitable for any other than the largest gardens. There are two types of bamboo, with different growth habits:

- **The clump-forming bamboos** (pachymorph rhizomes) are obviously the more desirable forms, because there are no noticeable runners or rhizomes to take over the rest of the property. The entire clump gradually expands with age – the giant bamboo so often seen growing along the coastal areas of KwaZulu-Natal is a typical, albeit large, example of a clump form.

- **The runner type of bamboo** (leptomorph rhizome) has extensive and very invasive rhizomes or runners and care must be taken to contain these runners if these bamboos are planted.

Indigenous vlei reed (*Phragmites australis*) and giant Spanish reed (*Arundo donax*), which is a declared weed, are not bamboos, although both are of the grass family.

There is a very limited range of properly identified bamboos in South Africa, and often when they are purchased little or no information is forthcoming as to how they will perform when planted. The clump forms available are ideal for medium to large garden spaces, where other than thinning out the old, dead and untidy

Cycas revoluta is a dramatic foliage plant for sun or semi-shade. It comes from Japan and should not to be confused with indigenous cycads

Where there is space, the majestic effect of bamboo can add interest and focus to a garden, and provide some handy canes too.

growth from time to time, little need be done except feed and water in the dry months. Remember that all bamboos are evergreen and need some water in the dry period. The runner varieties, including the amazing black bamboo (*Phyllostachys nigra*), can be planted in containers, where they will grow for years, if fed, thinned out from time to time and watered regularly. Make sure that the container is a reasonable size, at least 50 cm deep and wide. If planted in the garden they can be contained with a metal strip 20–30 cm wide and overlapped to totally surround the space allocated to the bamboo. The strip is dug into the ground with a centimetre or two showing above the surface. The stolons or runners are reasonably shallow and as they appear over the metal strip you simply cut them off. Breaking off any shoots as they appear above ground will also help to a degree.

Most bamboos only send out new growth in October/November, depending on the weather, and if proper control is exercised at that stage there is very little to do in terms of maintenance for the rest of the year. Periodically thin out old canes and, if necessary, chop away part of the clump to keep the plant under control. Bamboo appears to be totally disease resistant:

the only insect I have encountered on bamboo is mealy bug, which a systemic insecticide scattered on the surrounding soil seems to kill off.

PERENNIALS

Any plant that yearly repeats its previous season's performance in the garden can be regarded as perennial. This could imply that all trees and shrubs are perennial – true. But the general concept is that the above-ground parts of the plants die off at the end of each season, and are cut back, often to ground level, and reappear with each new growing season. Plants typical of this are *Dahlias*, *Hostas*, shasta and Michaelmas daisy and other similar plants. There are also evergreen perennials such as *Acanthus mollis* (wild rhubarb), hellebores, some violets (others are deciduous), *Agapanthus*, *Clivia*, and so on. Some perennials that are naturally evergreen become deciduous in cold areas – such as *Cannas*.

Perennials can be regarded as perfect fillers in any garden situation. They form the perfect transition from the permanent garden material – trees, creepers and shrubs – to the less permanent plants such as annuals, lawn,

and groundcovers. Their position in the garden is not fixed or rigid, and they can be used anywhere – which is ideal, as they have to be split up from time to time. Used among permanent trees and shrubs, annuals and ornamental grasses, they provide a typical full garden effect. On the other hand, they can be used as mass plantings in specific areas or isolated patches among more permanent material whilst this is growing to maturity. Taller perennials can be planted near the front of beds to add character; clumps can be added at the edge of pathways to provide a more permanent effect when annuals are being replaced, or they can simply be used to provide cut flowers during the various seasons.

Generally perennials prefer well-composted, well-drained, relatively deep soil. They are greedy feeders, particularly those that prefer not to be moved too often – *Peonies*, *Clivia* and hellebores, for example (they tend to sulk for a season or two once moved). In the case of plants that need to be split up on a regular basis, almost yearly, or at best, every two years, feeding is easy. It is simply a case of proper soil preparation each time they are moved, with liquid, organic or chemical fertilisers applied as needed during the

Red hot pokers, Kniphofia praecox, *are easy to grow, long-flowering perennials for any sunny position.*

A well-balanced planting of perennials will offer weeks, even months, of colour.

interim growing seasons. In the case of those deciduous perennials, such as *Peonies*, which are not happy if moved too often, the situation is a little trickier. The easiest is to mound the dormant plant with well-rotted kraal manure or compost during the winter months and foliar feed throughout the growing season. For the evergreen varieties that do not wish to be moved often, a trench the width of a spade can be dug far enough away from the roots so as not to impact on the growth of the plant, and filled with well-rotted manure or compost and fertiliser. This should be done just before the new growing season or very early on in the new season, preferably before the appearance of any new growth. A simpler method is to regularly scatter well-rotted kraal manure among the plants during their growing season: in fact, this is beneficial to any perennials.

To produce new plants, the older flowering plants can be lifted after they have finished flowering and not too near their next flowering period. The older parts of the plant are discarded and the new, young material is planted out. Plant at distances that will allow the plants to develop for a year or two without any further disturbance. In the case of plants that flower from the same point, year after year, such as *Agapanthus* and *Clivia*, the older material is planted – splitting off new, younger material from it and planting them as new plants. Don't divide slow-growing perennials into too many small clumps; they will take a long time to recover and be rather slow to come into flower again. Some perennials can be propagated by means of cuttings taken from the tips of new growth, once the initial softness of new growth has passed and the stems have not yet stretched into flower spikes. This is an easy way to propagate such perennials as *Chrysanthemums*, Michaelmas and shasta daisies.

Aftercare is simple in most cases: regular feeding, removing dead flower heads, watering properly during the growing season. In some cases the flowering is a seasonal event, but some perennials, if the old flower heads are cut back, will produce more flowers in the same season or later, before their dormant period. *Dahlias*, Inca lilies and some *Agapanthus*, day lilies and daisy varieties are typical examples of these.

Depending on the plant type, the pests and diseases are typical and common and can be treated accordingly. If the areas between the plants are mulched, retaining moisture and keeping the soil from compacting, many of the more typical problems can be overcome. A few common perennials have almost traditional problems – powdery mildew on perennial *Phlox* and *Dahlias*, dying off of *Gazanias*, vygies and *Arctotis*, rust on carnations and some violets. All of these are weather- and water-related; some seasonal, some poor drainage related. If your soil tends to retain water (clay soil), either add more sand for drainage or opt for plants that will tolerate the heavier, wet soil.

PESTS

Much has been written about pests and pest control. Numerous products fill the garden centre shelves. Simply put, all plants have some form of pest problem, and this will continue through the various phases of their development from new growth to setting of seed. It is almost impossible to have a pest-free garden, particularly in an urban situation, where the quality of garden care varies from property to property. The healthier the garden the less – or apparently less – impact pests will have on it.

Control methods are a lot simpler than most people realise:

DETERRENT METHODS involve planting or spraying extracts of plants that naturally repel pests by way of their aroma or taste. Garlic, rue, *Achillea*, *Artemisia*, lavender, khakibos, marigolds and *Nasturtiums* are some of the plants that can be used. This method will not kill any pests, but serves as a means of keeping them away. Because these are totally organic methods, respraying regularly after rain or watering is required.

ENVIRONMENTAL METHODS will have a low impact on the general environment but at the same time have the desired impact on specifically targeted pests. Some of them include natural chemicals, such as plant oils and extracts, formulated to have a specific effect as insecticides.

- Traps and bait covers placed in among plants protect the baits used, keeping them out of reach of bird and family pets.
- Containers filled with water and a little turpentine placed under a light in the garden will attract, collect and drown night-active beetles.
- Plastic bottles with small openings cut into their sides, containing a fruit-based mixture, hung among fruit trees will attract and collect fruit flies.
- Some plants act as host plants, and collect offending pests; one such plant is the marigold, which attracts eelworm or nematodes to its roots –

and at the end of the season the plants are pulled up and destroyed.

- Use mulching to keep areas damp: this helps to deter white fly and red spider mite.
- These and many other methods will help fight off bug infestations in a safer way.

CHEMICAL CONTROL is the most common method of pest control. This form of control is applied as contact poisons, which kill on contact with the insect, or as stomach poisons, which kill insects when they eat plants that have been sprayed. In both cases the correct dosage is important, as is the time lapse between applications. All pests have a specific life cycle, and to have a positive impact on this life cycle the insecticide must be sprayed at times relevant to it.

As pesticides are becoming more insect-specific, it is important that the correct product is used to have maximum effect. A wider range of insects is active during the warmer, growing months. Many of the winter-active pests are less detrimental and could be seen as almost harmless. There is one exception – the Mediterranean conifer aphid, which sucks sap out of the conifer whilst inserting a poisonous substance into the stem. The result is that in the early growing season, small areas of the conifer begin to die off. If the control is not applied during the later summer growing season it will be too late. For this there is a granular systemic insecticide that can be spread on the ground surrounding the plants, and is absorbed through the root system and into the structure of the plant before the pest becomes active. This insecticide is an ideal control method for many pests, without the fear of spraying chemicals into the air and onto clothing or skin. It cannot be over-emphasised that skin is as organic as plant surfaces are, and can be adversely affected when chemicals are being sprayed without the proper use of protective clothing.

pH

This is a term used when referring to the level of acidity or alkalinity in the soil. Meters and test kits to test the current pH levels in soil are available from many leading garden centres. A reading below 7 indicates that the soil is acidic (sometimes referred to as sour), and above 7 indicates that the soil is alkaline (sweet soil). Soil that is tested and shows a reading of 7 is regarded as neutral (neither the one thing or the other). As the majority of plants prefer a slightly acid soil, these tests are an indication of what needs to be done to correct the pH of the soil by way of feeding and chemicals.

Agricultural lime and alum can be added to soil to increase the pH and make it more alkaline.

Oak leaves, pine needles, iron chelate and Epsom salts can be added to soil to reduce the pH and make it more acid.

POISONOUS PLANTS

Although a number of plants are toxic in one way or another, it is important to see poisonous plants in a calm and logical light. There is little point in removing each and every garden plant that is identified as either deadly or mildly poisonous. Perhaps the important approach is that people, especially children, must be made aware of the possibility that any plant can be potentially harmful until proven otherwise.

- Children must be taught not to put foliage, flowers or fruit in their mouths.
- Hands and any other exposed skin should be washed after working in the garden.
- Don't cook food over a fire made from logs and kindling that is unknown.
- If plants have excessive sap, particularly milky sap, wear gloves when working with them.
- Wear protective clothing if the plants are particularly hairy or have rigid thorns.

CLOCKWISE FROM LEFT: Impala lily, Adenium multiflorum, *Ceylon's Rose,* Nerium oleander, *and Belladonna lily,* Amaryllis belladonna, *are all beautiful yet poisonous plants to be handled carefully.*

- Some plants can cause skin irritation when brushed against – have suitable medication on hand to treat such skin irritations.
- Have the number of the local poison centre handy.
- Know how to describe garden plants and in the event of ingestion take samples of the plant for identification if a visit to the doctor or hospital is necessary.

There is very comprehensive literature available on the subject of poisonous plants. Stay fully informed. There are surprisingly few deaths reported of people who have ingested poisonous plants, but don't take unnecessary risks.

POTTING SOIL

Although potting soil is readily available at any plant sales outlet, there are occasions when small amounts are needed or the bulk products are not up to expectations.

A simple medium can be made by mixing together 1 x compost; sifted, 1 x garden soil or milled wood bark, 1 x clean sand, not too fine. The measuring unit is irrelevant. If the medium needs to drain better, add more sand, and if it needs to retain more moisture add either more compost or water-retaining chemicals – use as directed.

Fertilisers can be added to the final mixed medium at the rate of 3 g each of all-purpose fertiliser and superphosphates per normal bucket-sized amount of medium.

PRUNING

Pruning is a means of controlling the size of a plant, assisting it to produce more flowering growth and encouraging or limiting fruit and seed production. Obviously there are various reasons and seasons when pruning is essential or advisable.

Pruning seasons

Winter is traditionally the time of the year when deciduous fruit trees are pruned. It is also an appropriate time to prune deciduous ornamental trees, when the shape and size of the tree structure can be clearly seen and assessed. Other plants that can be pruned in winter are those that will flower on new growth later in the growing season, such as roses, *Hydrangea*, pride of India and *Plumbago* or *Tecomaria* (*Tecoma*). Do not winter prune any plant material that will flower early in spring, unless it is to tidy up the shape of a plant that has been damaged. This will result in either very little flowering or none.

Late spring is the ideal time of the year to prune the late winter and early spring flowering plants.

Summer is the ideal time to regenerate growth of plants that have become untidy, straggly or bare at the base. It can encourage plants to flower again later in the season and can be used to repair seasonal storm damage. It is also an alternative time to prune spring-flowering material.

Reasons for pruning

- Reshape trees or shrubs after weather, machinery, people or animals have damaged their shape.
- Remove diseased wood from trees or shrubs.
- Lift lower branches of trees for access or to allow more light in under the tree.
- Encourage new growth, which will produce flowers and fruit.
- Encourage new growth, which will fill in woody areas of the plant.
- Artistically reshape the plant, e.g. hedges and topiary.
- Contain the natural shape of a plant that is too vigorous for the area, such as *Bougainvillea*, ivy or *Plumbago*.
- Cut back plants that have frosted or died off naturally in the winter months, e.g. tree ferns, wild bananas, *Strelitzia* or ornamental grasses.
- Generally tidy up the garden.
- Cut plants away from essential services such as gutters, telephone cables and streetlights.

Pruning is as important as feeding, watering and protecting plants against pests and disease. It is an ongoing aspect of gardening, which if left unattended will result in a garden that becomes overgrown and lacking in any form or healthy growth.

Points to remember
Keep pruning equipment sharp, sterile and well oiled.

If cutting off a large branch, first cut anywhere along the branch to reduce the weight, then cut the underside of the branch to prevent ripping of the bark, and finally cut from the top, downwards, where the branch extends from the trunk.

Cut branches off just beyond the swelling of the stem rather than at the stem. This will allow the tree to heal quicker.

When cutting thick branches, make sure they are sealed with a reliable tree sealer within two days of pruning.

Cut at a slight slope just above a bud when pruning generally.

Try to retain the natural shape of the plant when pruning to regenerate new growth.

Don't leave unnecessary twig or branch lengths (coat hangers) after pruning, as these are entry areas for diseases and woodborer.

Remove damaged branches as soon as possible to prevent the plant from becoming misshapen and possibly diseased through the damaged area.

When pruning woody shrubs that have become overgrown, try not to prune into the area where there are only bare stems. This applies particularly to plants that need to be pruned lightly and often, rather than severely, less often, e.g. *Erica*, *Protea*, lavender and rosemary. Begin by pruning, at random, a third of the growth, then wait until this pruned wood has developed leaves before pruning a further one third, wait again for leaf development and only then prune the remaining one third of the plant.

Properly 'geared' to mechanically cut or trim large plants (i.e. trees) is the safest and most efficient way to work.

Successful pruning can only be undertaken with well-cared-for pruning equipment suited to the task.

QUESTIONS AND HOW TO ASK THEM

In all gardens there comes a time when advice is sought. In many cases the incorrect information received is as a result of a badly asked question.

Points to remember and include in the questions asked

- Identify and clarify what answers are needed.
- Relate the questions to relevant areas or plants in the garden.
- Include aspects regarding size of space and plant/s.
- Enquire about growing conditions, position and after-care of a plant being considered.
- Mention surrounding plants relevant to the space or plant under discussion.
- Identify the microclimates in the garden space – exposed or protected areas.
- Find out about rates of growth and performance of new plants.
- What type/s of soil are on the property – drainage, acidity, etc?

(Colour is only a guide to a type of soil.)

- How many plants need to be planted together for an effect?
- What distance apart must the intended plants be planted?
- During which season should the plant be at its best?
- If plants are diseased or infested by insects, take samples for identification.

The more facts included in the questions asked, the more informative the answer will be. Information on the after-care of any new plant will be of long-term benefit to its well-being. Knowledge of plants' likes and dislikes as regards positioning, soil type, climate, rainfall and drainage will help create the ideal growing conditions for any newly introduced plant.

At the end of the day, the most important reason for asking questions correctly is that when a plant is purchased, as much information as possible should be gathered together to plant the correct plant in the correct position, using the correct planting procedure – and, once the plant is positioned, giving it the correct care. Incidentally, DIY aspects of gardening also require well-thought-out questions before you set to buying or building any non-plant aspects of your garden.

Nobody's too smart to ask questions, particularly in unfamiliar circumstances, or when trying out new plant combinations.

hedges. The Old English and heritage roses are a mixture of very old varieties and new hybrids typical of the old varieties. Highly scented, very full-petalled (at one time known as 'cabbage' roses), nostalgic, in soft dusty colours (there are some vivid coloured ones too), and an absolute must for English cottage gardens and as specimens in the large rambling 'farm'-styled gardens where their scent drifts on the late afternoon air.

CLIMBING AND STANDARD ROSES are more plant forms than specific rose types. Not all rose varieties are available as climbers, but among the vast range of climbing roses available there are hybrid teas and floribundas, as well as column or pillar roses; some ideal for arbours, others for walls, and, as the name implies, some can be grown up against a pillar or trained into a spire or column. Standard roses have been grafted onto taller under-stock than their bush counterparts: almost any rose could be grown as a standard if needed. Availability of standard roses is usually based on popularity, demand and the discretion of the rose grower.

Annual rose care

Summer care is simple: feed regularly with an appropriate fertiliser for flowering plants. Do this from the beginning of the growing season (August), at six-weekly intervals, until late autumn (April or May): 30–60 g per plant will suffice. If roses are grown in containers, feed once a month to replace nutrients flushed from the soil by watering. Liquid foliar feed applications are ideal for this purpose. Water thoroughly at least once a week; less if it rains. Make sure the plants' roots are cool and moist at all times – use an organic mulch to retain moisture and help keep roots cool. (See MULCH.) Don't dig among the roots during their growing months.

Remove dead flowers and lightly cut back the plant by roughly 20 cm after

A barren fence takes on a new look when covered with a climbing rose – and acquires added security too.

flowering to encourage new growth. New growth means new flowers. Regularly check for pests and diseases and treat accordingly. Remove damaged or dead wood as soon as possible. Remove any growth from below the graft, as this is not the variety purchased, but the under-stock onto which it has been grafted. For the same reason, this also applies to any growth that develops on the stem of standard roses.

Winter care of roses involves mostly pruning and removal of dead foliage. Dead foliage is removed because it is a likely place for fungus spores to over-winter. It simply helps to keep the general area around the roses healthy. There is no art to pruning: 'badly' pruned roses will recover and bloom as easily as roses that were pruned 'better'. Attend a few pruning and summer care demonstrations and invest in a good local book on the subject. Prune even if you are dubious or hesitant – just follow simple rules:

- Remove congested branches from within the shape of the plant. This

allows for air movement during the growing season and reduces fungal development.

- Remove dead, damaged and very old wood that has produced little or no new growth.

- Reduce the height of the plant to 50–30 cm, cutting growth just above an outward-facing bud. (Buds are found at the base of each leaf or leaf scar.)

- Prune even if roses still have the odd bloom or foliage in later winter.

- In extreme cases such as groundcover roses or miniatures (and some smaller-growing varieties of floribundas), cut back the bush with a pair of hedge clippers.

- When in doubt, cut off a little more than is felt to be necessary, the plant will re-grow and still bloom. Smaller is almost always better!

- If roses need to be moved, do it after pruning. Try and re-align them with north in their new positions.

- Spray with a recognised form of winter spray – either lime sulphur or an oil-based product.

SEED

 There is a mystery about seed that from time to time nudges people into attempting to germinate them. Throughout the seasons, numerous plants in any garden will set seed. These are often cut off or swept up and disposed of. Some fall and germinate *in situ* with little or no help from gardeners. Alternatively, there are increasingly more interesting seed types being sold in packets by reliable seed merchants for the adventurous gardener to grow.

Irrespective of how the seed is obtained, following a few pointers will make germinating it easier and more fun as well as providing plants that otherwise might have been costly or difficult to find.

- Identify the plants from which seed is to be collected before the seed is ripe. By doing this, information regarding the size, position and general appearance of the expected plant can be recorded in advance.

- Watch ripening seed closely, particularly if it is fine, wind distributed or attractive to birds, rodents or insects. This way the seed may be protected or safely contained before being eaten or dispersed.

- If seed is to be contained to prevent loss, make sure the method used allows free air passage as well as good light for ripening. Don't use plastic bags to cover ripening seed; this could cause rotting or fungal diseases. An ideal method is to cut the foot piece off a stocking and carefully pull this over the ripening seed head. If the plant is annual and dying off as the seed ripens, remove the entire plant and tie the heads inside paper bags; the plants are then hung upside down until the seed ripens and falls from the plants into the bag.

- Make sure the date of collection and the name of the plant are written on the bag or container used to store seed. Store seed in an airtight

Larger seeds are easy to sow and best planted individually because they can be slow to germinate.

container – *once* it has dried properly. This will prevent it from developing mildew, other fungal or insect problems. A light dusting with a powdered fungicide or flowers of sulphur will help keep seed healthy.

- Do not keep seed too long before sowing – sow in the following growing season of that plant. Summer-flowering seed harvested in late summer or autumn (e.g. marigold, *Salvia* or *Impatiens*) – sow during the next spring. Winter and spring flowering seed harvested in late spring (*Primula*, African daisy or *Cosmos*, perhaps) can be sown in late summer.

- If the seed has a fleshy coating (such as *Clivia*, *Crinum*, *Asparagus* or any other soft berry types), remove the coating before sowing immediately or drying and storing. Don't plant too deep; the top 1/3 of the seed should be visible.

- Most tree and shrub seeds mature and ripen in autumn and can safely be sown immediately, although some will only germinate in the following spring. Alternatively, seed can be stored as mentioned and sown in spring.

- Most packaged seed is made available during the ideal sowing season. Where applicable, check to see that the seed packet is date stamped, indicating the life of the seed. Don't buy old seed.

- Check to see that sound, relevant advice is on each packet of seed purchased. Avoid generalised information.

- To test some of the larger, harder seeds – cycads, acorns or nut-like seeds – for viability, drop them into a bucket of water: those that float will not grow; those that sink, will (or should)!

Methods of sowing at home

Generally, flower and vegetable seed can be broadcast over an open area in the garden, covered with a little soil, watered – and most of them will grow. This applies to a wide range of readily available seed as well as that usually harvested from garden annuals and perennials. Some of the more select seed needs to be grown in seedbeds or seed trays so as to exercise optimum control over growing conditions in the early stages.

Broadcasting seed

Dig over the area well, digging in compost and general balanced fertiliser at the rate of 30 g per square metre. Rake the area lightly. Scatter the seed, not too close together, but close enough to give a full effect when the plants mature. Re-rake the area lightly, and water well. Don't allow the area to dry out, but if drainage is poor don't water too often either. Avoid walking over the area when sown; rather allow open areas among the sown areas where you can stand to water and weed (or, if the area is large, create informal, narrow, earth pathways among the sowings). Don't water during the heat of the day.

Seedbeds

A more controlled situation than the garden space method, but similar in other respects. Select an area in the garden and prepare a workable patch no wider than a metre – or any width that can be cared for from either side without walking into the bed; length is immaterial. Prepare the area as discussed above and sow the seeds in rows or broadcast evenly over the area. If seed is sown in rows, keep the rows at least 10–20 cm apart. Lightly cover seed with sifted, dry potting soil and water well. The area can be covered with a piece of hessian or newspaper before watering. This is kept on until the seeds germinate.

Once the seed has germinated and seedlings have at least two pairs of mature leaves, plant out into other areas of the garden. They will wilt, but can be covered with paper cups or cones until they have established themselves. In the case of vegetables sown in rows, thin out and where practical (not carrots), transplant the thinned-out plants, allowing the remaining plants enough space to develop *in situ*.

Seed trays

This is the most specialised homeowner method of growing seed. Seeds can be sown in individual pots or rows, or broadcast in a situation where almost total control can be exercised over their treatment and conditions. Anything can be used as a seed tray, as long as it will not fall apart before the seed is planted out.

- Place the seed tray anywhere there is good light and air circulation, no build up of heat or draught and the sown seed will not be washed away by rain. Specific domestic problems must be taken into account – family pets, play areas or family activities do not make ideal seed tray areas.

- Fill the seed trays with a slightly damp, sifted potting soil (in some areas seed sowing mixtures are available), to just below the top of the tray. Minimum depth should be 5 cm, and good drainage is important.

- Gently firm the soil down into the seed tray and level it off. Do not over-compact the soil. If potting soil is not used, a mixture of one part topsoil, one part clean sand and one part compost or leaf mould will suffice. Sift this through a reasonably fine sieve.

Seed sowing is more successful if a sturdy seed-sowing tray is used, but durable alternatives will work as well.

- Sow seed, making sure the seed is covered with as much soil as the thickness of the seed as it lies naturally on the seed tray surface. (Seed packets indicate how deep to sow seed.) Large seeds are best planted alone or spaced well apart in rows.

- Cover the surface with a piece of hessian or newspaper before watering – keep this on until seed begins to germinate. Don't let the surface dry out.

Hint: An entire seed tray can be slipped inside a clear plastic bag such as a freezer-bag and sealed until the seed germinates.

- Once the seedlings reach a manageable size, plant them out into either their final position or further seedling trays until better established. Evergreen plant seed should be sown in such a way as not to disturb the roots too often – individual pots, perhaps. Handle young developing seedlings with care when planting them out into other situations, as they damage easily.

Points to remember

- It is seldom necessary to feed germinating seed – rather plant into well-fed soil. Slow-growing tree and shrub seed that may grow in the seedbed for a long time may need to be fed from time to time – use a liquid organic fertiliser for this.

- Don't weed *in situ* sowings too early, unless the germinating seed is easily identifiable.

- Sow several seed trays rather than overcrowding one tray if lots of a specific plant are needed. Sow only what is required, and reseal the remainder of the seed, either for a later sowing or to replace a failed sowing.

- Don't freeze seed unless it helps with germination; it could damage the embryo (germination point) –

A well-balanced shrub planting adds permanent character to the garden.

rather keep it at the bottom of the fridge.

- Some tree and shrub seed has a soft fleshy coating encasing the seed or seeds. Remove this coating when preparing the seed for drying, storing or sowing, as in some cases the chemical content of this coating can damage or inhibit the germination of the seed.

SHRUBS

The most important group of plants in any garden! Shrubs provide screening, colour, contrast and a permanent background to other plants. They range from low groundcovering plants to large, tree-like specimens.

Maintenance of shrubs is quite simple: get to know them and what they need – in other words, their *plant profile*. This covers size, position, soil preference, hardiness, sun/shade tolerance, evergreen/deciduous, flowering (and if so, when), water requirements, when to feed and with what, how and when to prune, whether they are long-lived or not, poisonous, quick- or slow-growing, bear fruit or not, and so on.

Aspects of a plant profile

Size
This is generally the natural size a plant will grow to as it matures. Both height and width are important. Many plants are kept to a man-made size for reasons such as functionality, space available and desired effect. Shrub care will depend on knowing a plant's final size, if it can be pruned smaller or not, and when and how often to do so.

Position
Generally this refers to where in the garden the shrub is planted; however, it should relate to neighbouring plants as well. Position will determine how the plants stand up to the weather – frost, heat, hail and rain. Position will also relate to the nature of the terrain – level or a slope, stony, clay, sandy or ideal loam.

Soil preference
Soil is either acid or alkaline (sweet); less often is it neutral. The means of measuring is called pH. Although most plants will grow well in almost any kind of soil type, there are some that have definite preferences. Blue *Hydrangeas* will only stay blue if the soil is acid; yellowing of leaves is often caused by soil being too alkaline for a particular plant's growing

requirements – typical of this situation are *Gardenia*, *Azalea* and *Camellia* – all of these will develop yellow foliage (chlorosis) if soil is not acid enough.

Sun or shade?
Although many plants will tolerate a change in the quantity of sun as the shadows lengthen or recede during the day, there are those that will perform best if kept consistently in their preferred position. For example, cacti and succulents must grow in full sun, whilst sensitive shade-loving ferns will react badly if exposed to direct sunlight. Quite a few general garden plants will be able to grow well if they receive sufficient light – good daylight, not necessarily sunlight. This is important, as in most gardens the plants create a form of shade, which, as they develop, excludes direct sunlight to smaller plants nearby.

Evergreen or deciduous?
All plants will lose leaves from time to time – in some cases, such as palm trees, this may only occur every few months or years. Other plants will lose all their foliage annually – in autumn. Other 'evergreen' plants will lose a percentage of their foliage if and when the plant comes into flower – typical of this are *Brunfelsia* (yesterday, today and tomorrow), *Ligustrum* species (privet) and *Sterculia acerifolia* (Australian flame tree). Many plants, although permanently evergreen, constantly drop old, dying leaves as new foliage develops – for example, *Eucalyptus*, conifers, *Melaleuca* and bottlebrushes. To avoid gaps in the garden, it is important to know into which category the plants fall.

Do the plants flower?
Some plants are not grown for their flowers, but rather for another aspect of their appearance – the white stem of birches or lavender-wood, bold foliage of a *Philodendron* or multi-coloured foliage of a *Coprosma* or *Croton*. If a plant is chosen for its flowers, know when to expect these and for how long they will last – spring flowering plants seldom flower for any great length of time, because the weather heats up too quickly. Are the flowers significant, or do they need added, similar colour nearby to accentuate them? Are the seeds or fruit more spectacular than the flowers? (In which case flowering needs to be encouraged to provide these second-phase effects.)

Watering and feeding
These two should go hand in hand, so it is important to know when and how to

The use of the white birches, Betula alba, *receding through the shrubbery gives great depth to what is a reasonably small space.*

To create interest and depth in a shrubbery, combine various foliage colours, sizes and textures.

lifespan. This means that constant attention must be given to such plants, while the short-lived plants perhaps require less attention, particularly as regards feeding and pruning.

Poisonous plants
There is a growing awareness of plants' poisonous potential, encouraged by valuable publications and website information. Not all poisonous plants have to be removed and destroyed, not at all, but there is peace of mind to be had from up-to-date knowledge.

With this wealth of knowledge regarding each plant at hand, garden maintenance is simply a matter of doing the right thing at the right time. Remember that when using shrubs it is important to be aware of their performance over a whole 12-month cycle. Not all plants can be treated in the same way, at the same time of year. The feeding, watering and pruning applied must be relevant to the specific shrub, their needs, your expectations and the season.

Points to remember
- Prune from a young age, maintaining a good natural shape: this prevents bare, leafless lower sections of the shrub as it matures.

- Don't disturb or dig around plants unnecessarily: this damages roots, dries the soil out and retards growth. In select cases, such as *Protea* and *Leptospermum* species, the plants can die.

- Even if the shrub is small when first planted, don't place it too close to other plants; allow space for each shrub to develop a reasonable natural shape and size.

- Feed regularly during the growing season, every 6 weeks, from August to April.

- Plants that need feeding during the normally dormant period from May to August (especially winter-flowering shrubs), should be fed with a foliar feeder rather than a granular fertiliser.

- Don't over-water established shrubs: they should be able to support

apply both. Too little food or too much water may have an adverse effect on the plant's performance. For example, *Bougainvillea* prefers dry, under-fed conditions to flower well, while *Camellia* will not flower well at all if not fed and watered during autumn and winter. Water is a valuable commodity and it is important to provide the plant with the desired amount – but not to waste water either. Similarly, knowing what and when to feed a plant means that the plant will benefit, but fertiliser will not be wasted.

Lifespan of a plant
Not all plants live for the same amount of time: some, annuals for example, have a very short lifespan. Some of the Cape 'fynbos' only lives a few years and dies off. If these plants are used in the garden, it is important to know what can be expected from them and for how long. *Ensete ventricosa* (wild banana) will grow well for 6–8 years, then having flowered, will begin to die. (Removing the flower will not increase their life span at all.) Other plants such as *Camellia* and holly have an indefinite

themselves during normal dry periods and seasons.

- Don't under-water plants forming buds or beginning to set fruit, especially if this happens during a dry period – citrus often begin to set fruit in late winter. *Camellias*, flowering quinces, almonds, some *Pelargoniums*, *Proteas*, *Ericas* and *Azaleas* flower in winter, before the beginning of the summer rains. Similarly, in the winter rainfall regions there are summer-flowering plants that will require extra attention as they come into flower during the dry summer months.

- Plants from winter rainfall areas, but propagated under summer rainfall region conditions – *Proteas* and *Ericas*, for example – need no special treatment and can be treated like any other shrubs grown locally. This applies in the reverse too, that plants originally from summer rainfall areas can readily adapt to growing in the winter rainfall regions if tested and propagated there.

- Conifers planted too close to each other or other plants will die off where they touch the other plants. This also applies when annuals, perennials or groundcovers are allowed to grow up into their lower branches. Seldom do these dead areas produce new growth once this has happened.

- Where possible, try to group plants that have similar needs of watering and soil conditions together. (See WATER-WISE GARDENING)

- Don't plant shrubs too close too walls or other solid structures, as they will tend to grow away from the wall as they mature. This also applies to shrubs planted under the roof overhang.

- Remove all labels, plant ties and stakes from new plants when planting. Stake only if necessary.

- Take care not to plant plants too deep or too shallow. Rather allow a hollow for watering – which can be filled in once the shrub is established.

When plants have to be supported, avoid pushing a stake through the root ball; rather use two stakes, one on either side of the root ball, and support the plant between them. In windy situations, these stakes should be inserted in the direction of the prevailing winds for best support.

By using the plants in combination with the right accessories or hard landscape elements different effects can be obtained.

SOIL CARE

Although soil preparation has been dealt with under headings such as fertilisers, manure, compost and nutrients, I think that there is a need to discuss the care of soil in general – before or after feeding and organic boosting.

Soil is simply a collection of large to ultra-small rock particles, and is in itself simply a means of holding roots firmly in place. It may be clay or sandy – or, in an ideal world, a perfect combination of both, called loam – but other items held between the stone particles determine the quality of the soil as a growing medium. Keeping this 'soil' healthy is not simply a question of feeding and watering it; it is more a question of what to do and not to do with the medium itself.

Don't ...
- dig over the beds unnecessarily – this dries out the soil and kills off beneficial bacteria and enzymes.

- walk in areas once they have been prepared for planting – this compacts the soil and makes it more difficult to keep moist.

- add fertiliser and compost if the plants are dormant – this will be depleted by the time the plants are active and need feeding.

- water superficially – this helps to form a compacted crust of the upper soil, encourages shallow root development and makes it difficult for water to penetrate.

- dig in raw organics such as lawn clippings or leaves unless extra nitrogen is applied to compensate for the loss of available nitrogen during decomposition of the organics.

- remove rocks and pebbles – these are part of the soil structure and help with drainage.

Do ...
- mulch on an on-going basis – this keeps the soil cool, damp and inhibits weed development.

- remember to feed well at the beginning of the growing season (spring), when plant growth is vigorous.
- add inorganic elements such as washed sand, fine gravel or power station ash to improve drainage.
- encourage earthworms – for improved soil quality.
- water well but not more often than the specific plants require.
- remember to dig deep enough when preparing soil areas for planting.

SPRAYING

Irrespective of what plants are to be sprayed with, it is important to remember some basic, important aspects regarding spraying and spray equipment.

- Before spraying, check all spray equipment for leaks, broken seals, etc.
- ***Make sure that the person doing the spraying has the correct safety accessories, such as gloves, goggles, protective clothing and footwear***.
- Follow ALL instructions on any spray product container. Do not re-use any spray product containers; rather destroy them. (Break, flatten, cut up, or use any other method that renders the containers useless.) Discard any residue in a hole in the garden, rather than flushing it down the drain.
- Where possible, do not spray above eye level, or eat, drink or smoke whilst working with spray products.
- Make sure that all instructions are understood and that necessary antidotes are available should there be any excessive contact or ingestion of products.
- This is not an ideal world, and the question often asked is: 'If these products are so dangerous, why spray at all?' Gardeners will carry on spraying for one reason or another – and even if the products are not dangerous, it is better to be cautious than sorry.

- ***Always have the poison centre or crisis centre number handy***.
- Keep all spraying equipment, safety clothing and accessories and spray products out of the reach of all people not aware of their uses, application and dangers (particularly children, domestic staff and elderly people).
- No spraying equipment should have a secondary use. Keep weedkiller spray equipment clearly marked and separate from other more general equipment.
- Look for environment-friendly alternatives where possible, when purchasing products.
- Spray on clear, warm, wind-free days, but not during the heat of the day. Should it rain soon after spraying, wait 24 hours and spray again.
- If there is ever any doubt about the use, safety, shelf life or dosage of any product, contact the manufacturers.

Note: In all cases where the product is not clearly explained on the container or pamphlet, contact the manufacturer.

Some explanations of spray product terminology

Systemic – enters into the system of the plant through roots, stem and foliage. It works from the inside outwards. It has the same effect on skin!

Contact – usually refers to insecticides or fungicides that kill the insects or controls the fungal problem on contact (either the insect or fungi spores coming into contact with the product, or the product covering the insect).

Stomach poison – a product sprayed onto the foliage, which when eaten, along with the foliage or flower, will kill the insect.

Herbicide – a weed killer (an overall description).

Non-selective herbicide – will kill any plant it comes into contact with. Some of these are systemic and others are

Spraying can be hazardous and hard work, so it's important to use correct, manageable spraying equipment at all times.

contact sprays for the control of soft new growth (seasonal weeds).

Selective herbicide – designed to control or destroy a specific plant or range of plants growing among other plant types.

Fungicide – systemic or contact product that prevents or controls the development of fungal and bacterial problems in plants. (Some fungicides are selective for control of specific problems or on specific plant types.)

Wettable powder – a product available in a powder form that mixes readily with water, to be used as a drench or a spray.

Incompatible product – a product that cannot be mixed with other chemicals or control products.

Aphidicide – a product designed exclusively for the control of various aphid species.

Environmentally friendly – a product that has little or no negative impact on the environment in general, but addresses the problem. In some cases these are organic based, have a very short shelf life, and often need to be re-applied after watering or rain.

Biodegradable – means that the product is reduced by sunlight/weather (UV) from a solid product to something more environmentally acceptable.

Summer oil (otherwise known as **oleum**) – an oil-based product that may be mixed with water and applied for the control of insects on evergreen material. It is now recommended as a winter spray alternative to lime sulphur.

SUCCULENTS AND CACTI

Although plants from the arid parts of the world are generally easy to grow, a few helpful tips may enable you to enjoy them a lot more. From time to time these wonderfully odd-shaped plants surge in popularity – and like so many other 'fad' plants, people buy them without knowing just how to care for them. Generally easy plants to grow, they make great plants for kids who don't have access to a garden area but want to grow something. Cacti can be slow growing, and often they are killed by over-watering in the hopes that more water will help them grow quicker!

All cacti are in fact succulents, except they have spines (or thorns) that protrude

In areas that are important yet difficult to maintain cacti can be an ideal plant choice, especially if combined with the right accessories.

Because most succulents and cacti need limited root space they can be grown effectively in quite small or very shallow containers.

from a pattern of areoles or 'pincushions' specifically arranged all over the plant. The spines vary in shape, colour and size. All are rigid and some readily detach themselves if brushed against (quite a painful experience!) Almost all cacti originate in the Americas and do not have any leaves to speak of. Succulents are far more widely distributed than cacti; many of them are indigenous to southern Africa. Some, like *Euphorbia ingens* or *E. cooperi*, two forms of the naboom or candelabra tree, are in fact very dense trees of quite large proportions. They generally have fleshy leaves, which are sometimes waxy-coated or covered in a fine felt-like coating. This is nature's way of reducing evaporation. Succulents and cacti all have quite vivid flowers in the early part of the growing season.

Although cacti come from generally arid regions, they will react positively to a liquid foliar feeding at the beginning of each new growing season. Don't over-water, especially during the naturally dry season (usually winter), but if the drainage is good they can be planted in the garden. If grown indoors they need strong sunlight, and water every 14 days – pour off excess water from the drip tray directly after watering.

If planted as garden plants, because of the difficulty of weeding and cleaning between them I suggest that you grow them apart from other garden plants whose maintenance is easier – they are ideal for hot, dry window-boxes or similar planters. To make life even easier, plant them through holes cut into a sheet of plastic laid over the soil, and when firmly planted cover the plastic with fine gravel or pebbles. Wear gloves! Or wrap the plant in a collar of folded newspaper until it is firmly in place. If cacti are to be transplanted, a well-drained soil mixture that includes some sifted compost or leaf mould as well as coarse sand for drainage would be ideal. I have seen a cactus soil mix available as a ready-mixed item.

Many succulents can be propagated by splitting them up as one would perennials, and replanting them. The large single-stemmed cacti cannot be propagated in any other way than by harvesting and sowing seed. Many of them will grow quite large with time, and some take a long while to reach flowering size. Both succulents and cacti are prone to scale, mealy bug (especially among their roots), aphids and to a lesser extent red spider mite and thrips. See PESTS for control.

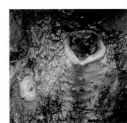

TOOLS

Garden tools are constantly being designed to make the lot of the gardener an easy one – but all too often the lifespan of the garden tool is shortened by a lack of care and attention. This often makes the task at hand more difficult or lengthy. Constant care of garden tools is not only important – it's essential!

Tool care advice

■ Buy quality garden tools, cheap ones don't last. Make sure that replaceable parts are available, and enquire if the suppliers or manufacturers have a service and repair facility. Tools sold under a guarantee are generally of a superior quality. If blades are chipped or blunt can they be sharpened, replaced or repaired?

■ Make sure that all users of any motorised garden tools know what fuel is used and where to put the required fuel, especially if oil and fuel have different tanks.

■ If the tools are electrical, check cables regularly to make sure that there are no nicks, cracks or exposed wires. If they are operated from outdoor power points, check these points regularly to ensure that the all-weather seals are intact and effective. If the tools are motorised, make sure that they are serviced regularly.

■ Any garden tools with blades for cutting trees or shrubs should be sterilised regularly, so that possible diseases are not transmitted from one plant to another. Wash and dry off manual garden tools after use to avoid rusting.

■ The seals in pressure sprayers should be checked if the sprayer has not been used for a long period of time, to make sure that they don't leak. Preferably, use a different pressure spray for each type of spray used – one for herbicides, another for insecticides, and so on. Each one should be clearly marked.

■ If a lawnmower is to be used during the winter months to help reduce dry, dead, lawn 'thatch', check the blades and service the machine *after* this.

■ Saw blades should cut through branches without tearing or snagging the wood or bark; if this is not the case they probably need sharpening or replacing.

■ Filters in water feature pumps should be cleaned regularly to ensure an easy flow of water. Check for wear and tear on impellors; make sure that replaceable parts for pumps are available.

Finally, make sure that all who use any form of garden tool, manual or mechanical, know exactly *how* to use it and *what* it is to be used for. If need be, arrange for users to attend a course with the manufacturers or suppliers before being allowed to use the more high-tech equipment.

TOPIARY

Simply put, this can be described as artificial shapes created with plants either by clipping them or by training them over metal or wood forms. Practised throughout the history of gardening, they come and go through various garden style periods. Usually topiary plants are linked with formal or architectural styles of garden design and the material used has to be able to survive and tolerate regular clipping. Generally, the ideal plants to choose for topiary are those with numerous small leaves on small close-set branches, an easy branching habit once clipped, showing a tendency towards a natural compact growth habit, and preferably evergreen.

A properly clipped 'Spiral' conifer in a well-chosen container adds elegance to this entrance.

Developing a topiary plant is simple. Decide whether the desired shape is to begin at ground level or grown on a standard; select the preferred plant type, choose a position and plant it. This could either be into a container or into the garden.

If the plant has to be grown from a cutting – perhaps nothing suitable can be purchased or there is a desire to experiment with a new plant, it is necessary to decide early on what shape the plant will finally have and prune or stake it accordingly. If the plant is intended to grow as a standard, determine the height and carefully select a strong central stem, encouraging it to grow straight up by staking the new growth until it reaches the desired height. Regularly cut off all side growth, retaining about one third of the top growth. Once the desired height has been reached, nip out the central growing point, which encourages it to begin branching. This process could take a season or two, depending on the rate of growth and the desired height of the standard. On the other hand, if the plant is to be grown from soil level, it is

an idea to allow the cutting to root, begin growing and early on lightly nip back the growing tips to encourage branching. In either case, once there are sufficient branches to begin forming the desired topiary shape, clip as required.

Don't be too perturbed should the shape initially not be quite as intended. This can be corrected by allowing parts of the plant to grow further before any more clipping, or by reshaping areas previously clipped incorrectly. A secret to successful topiary is regular clipping, removing small amounts of growth each time. Once the plant has acquired the desired shape and size, it is important to maintain this size and not allow the plant to grow increasingly larger. This may mean that every second or third growing season the plant has to be clipped further back than the intended size, and followed with regular clipping after that.

It is important to remember that container-grown topiary plants cannot be allowed to dry out ever, and that to encourage new growth, regular feeding will be essential. Another important aspect to remember for standardised

Clipped continuity needs to be carefully monitored and cared for – spot the odd one out.

topiary plants is that they must be constantly well staked until the plant is strong enough to stand alone. If the potted topiary plants stand close to a wall or other plant material it is a good idea to turn them slightly every two to three months to avoid the less full 'back' to the shape.

TREES

Trees are the largest plants in any garden situation and it is wise to remember that they require as much space below ground as they do above. Before selecting one, verify what it does – evergreen, deciduous, wide-spreading, slow- or fast-growing, and so on. Maintaining trees is relatively simple once they are established.

Trees have a large root system – not to be confused with an invasive root system. Most trees will develop a root system that keeps abreast with the aboveground growth. Should some of the larger roots begin to grow too near the surface, they can be cut out. This will encourage new, thinner roots to develop. Not all trees' roots will have an adverse impact on the surrounding surfaces.

Hint: In situations where there is a possibility of surface root damage or disturbance, try planting a young tree into a submerged section of storm-water pipe (50 cm diameter and a minimum of 60 cm into the soil); this encourages roots to penetrate deeper into the soil and the chance of disturbing the surface is drastically reduced.

Remember that trees, like all other plants, develop a circular crown – not a half or quarter of a circle. Don't plant trees too close to a boundary line or into a corner: use the entire size and shape of the tree in an area that can be controlled by you!

Maintaining new trees

If the tree is exposed to wind, is willowy and supple or not too straight, plant two wood or metal stakes at the same time as the tree is planted (one on either side of the root ball, in line with the direction of the wind); or if the tree has been planted, hammer them in, no further than 20 cm either side of the trunk. Do not tie the tree directly to the stakes. With the aid of tree ties or other material that will not damage the bark, tie it firmly between the stakes, keeping the tree upright.

Trim away all young growth from the stem, if this has not been done, allowing two thirds of the stem to be clean. If there are two or more stems, select the most upright and vigorous, and carefully remove the others at the point where they join. If a less formal tree shape is desired, several or all of these stems may be retained and trimmed up to the desired height or heights. It is wise to remember that trees with a natural multi-branching habit should be trained with two to five stems rather than persistently attempting to maintain a single stem. Some *Rhus* (karee) species are typical of this growth pattern.

Hint: Side branches are produced from a light swelling of the main stem. When trimming them off, do not cut into the swelling region, but rather just behind it. This encourages a healthy regrowth of the bark and healing is quicker. This pruning is generally done once a season only: if the tree is deciduous, do it during winter; or for evergreen trees, just before the beginning of the new growing season.

Although trees have large roots, some of which are more surface orientated than others and in some cases more invasive than others, it must be remembered that trees are not bad for structures – it is more a case of some structures not being strong enough to withstand the natural activities of trees. Often this is because the tree is planted too near these structures, whether they are walls, foundations, ponds, paving or piped services.

When planting a tree it is important to know what type of root system one can anticipate, how soon it will develop and how near the surface. This helps in placing the right tree in the right position. Remember that tree and shrub roots will quite naturally be drawn towards moisture, whether it is naturally available in the soil or from a leaking tap, fractured join in water piping or

By knowing the trees' growing habits and sizes, it's easy to know how far apart they can be planted. This is a young, man-made Betula alba *forest.*

sewer line, or from a water feature – including swimming pools that have not been built properly. Stories abound regarding the damage that willows will do to features in the garden, but seldom are the facts made known as to how poorly or how near to the base of the tree the features were built.

It is safe to assume that in most cases, the vigorous feeding roots are concentrated in line with the drip-line of the tree (its outer size and shape similar to the shadow cast at midday by the tree). The larger roots, which generally extend beyond the size of the tree, are those that have developed as anchoring roots. Should the need arise to sever or cut through one or more of these roots, little or no long-term impact will be apparent, as their role as producer of feeder roots will be taken on by other roots, or new roots will develop behind the cut-off root (although generally thinner) and the feeding process will continue. It is not wise to assume that all roots of all trees can be cut if they become problematic. Rather be advised by an expert as to which trees will take root pruning and which ones won't. In any event, it is unwise to remove more than 30 per cent of the offending root system at any one time, allowing up to 12 months before removing further roots. If large roots are cut through or shaved off, it is a good idea to allow the wound to be exposed for a day or two, to dry out, and then treat it with a tree sealant and cover with a piece of sheet plastic before re-covering with soil. This minimises the chances of fungal infection passing into the plant system from the surrounding soil or water. Be warned that some trees will sucker at the point where roots are cut and a greater problem could arise (poplars, elms, *Acacia melanoxylon* (blackwood), *Alianthus* and *Robinia* are among those known to do this).

Much has been said about which trees have taproots and which have a spreading root system. Irrespective of whether a tree has a taproot or not, there will be roots spreading outwards – firstly to anchor the tree and secondly to assist with the absorption of plant nutrients from the surrounding soil. A taproot is more the initial root development as the tree grows, and in the case of some trees – palms for example – this will develop and grow to great depths before any further root development takes place. As the tree develops so too will other roots.

Care of older, established trees

As trees develop, they often take on shapes that are not altogether acceptable, and need to be reduced in size, cut up to allow in more light, or trimmed into a more acceptable shape. In some cases these options arise as a result of wind or storm damage, alterations to structures (extending the home, for example), interference with overhead services or in the name of good neighbourliness.

Tree trimming can be hazardous, and cause untold damage to surrounding structures or other trees and shrubs if not done properly and with the correct equipment. Initially the first step should be to consult with pruning experts, tree surgeons or arboriculturists.

Though costly (in most cases) there is a chance that such aspects as insurance,

A properly cut branch healing effectively. Note totally healed wound on the left.

medical costs, etc. will be covered by a quotation and the onus of safety rests with the professional. Call for more than one quotation to be on the safe side.

The less expensive and less professional route is the home DIY system. This can result in the use of inadequate equipment and unsafe techniques, and plants can suffer as a result of this. Cost is a very real factor and when all aspects are being considered there are a few pointers that can be taken into consideration.

- Make sure that all equipment used is in perfect working order, saws are sharp and hoists, ladders and any cables or ropes used are whole, safe and able to reach the area to be worked in.

- Rather than allow heavy sections of cut branches to fall and damage other plants, tie a rope to the section being cut, throw it over another branch nearby or above, and use it to lower the cut section slowly to the ground.

- In cases where safety clothing or equipment (such as goggles, ear muffs, gloves or boots) is necessary, use them – don't think they are only designed for sissies.

- Consider the plant material to be removed or trimmed. Where will the safest place be to stand, and where can the cut-off material fall without unnecessary damage to property or other plants? Decide these things before cutting and felling any material.

- If material to be cut is too long or weighty, perhaps several smaller sections should be cut off instead of one large piece.

- Always undercut a branch where it grows from the main stem before cutting from the top. This prevents the weight of the branch from ripping the bark as it falls from the tree.

- Don't rest support equipment such as ladders against branches that are to be removed. Don't sit on the pieces to be removed!

- Never cut into the main trunk of the tree, unless the tree is to be removed totally. Always cut just beyond the swelling where branches grow out from one another.

- Try where possible to cut branches at a slight slope. This will prevent water from gathering on the cut area, perhaps resulting in rotting as the water soaks into the exposed surface.

- Allow any large cut surfaces to dry for a day or two before coating them with a reliable tree sealer. Make sure that these cut surfaces are free from bruised, jagged edges. Trim clean with a sharp knife, if necessary, before applying the sealer.

- It is advisable to trim trees when they are either totally without foliage, or (in the case of evergreen trees) before the beginning of a new growing season. It is easier to see the overall shape of the tree when there are fewer or no leaves.

- Even if shaping is not necessary, it is advisable to periodically tidy up the tree by removing any dead or damaged branches and sealing these cuts as described.

- Trees that are more dead than alive are best removed. Their reasons for dying could be old age (in the case of short-lived trees), a lightning strike, fungal disease or something similar. There is a chance that they could fall over or fall apart if any noticeable new growth is encouraged by pruning, which could enhance wind resistance.

- Finally, the simplest form of maintenance is to make sure that the right tree is planted in the right place from the beginning.

Tree feeding

One tends not to see a tree as something that needs feeding often, particularly once it has been established for a few years. In fact, to feed large trees becomes something of an arduous task, as often the feeding roots under the drip line have moved in under paving, flower beds or fixed structures or into neighbouring properties.

In the early stages of tree establishment, feeding is simple. General balanced fertilisers can be applied, as in the case of any other plants in the garden. There are slow-release tablets available that are pushed into the ground near the stem at the time of planting, and these are able to feed the tree for two to three years, thus ensuring sound establishment of the plant. As the roots spread out into the surrounding area, generally there are sufficient nutrients in the soil to maintain good growth. The problem arises when trees are older and reaching maturity and there are fewer newly developed feeding roots, spreading at a slower rate, and the tree has to rely on the depleted soil it has grown through over several years.

Foliar spraying is not practical in many cases, due to the size of the tree. In cases where access to most of the drip line is possible, 3–5 cm holes can be made, 50 cm deep, 50 cm apart in a 2-metre band (one metre inside and one metre outside of the drip line). Into these holes is poured a mixture of one part sand, one part balanced fertiliser and one part superphosphates. Pour the dry mix into the holes and water well. Similarly a trench could be dug, 50 cm deep, in a 2-metre-wide band under the drip line, and a mixture of one part well-rotted manure and one part soil could be used to fill it, adding 90 g super-

The 'forest' effect needs constant feeding, care and attention.

phosphates to each square metre of the surface of the trench.

Treatment for pests and diseases in large trees can be difficult and perhaps costly. A simple method is to drill several 1 cm holes into the trunk of the tree, a metre above ground level. The holes, roughly 20 cm apart, should encircle the tree and be drilled at a slight slope downwards. The insecticide or fungicide is mixed as indicated on the container and carefully poured (or syringed) into these holes. The holes can be plugged with cotton wool. At two- to three-day intervals check the level of fluid in the holes and continue filling up until the entire batch of the mixture is finished. This method will only prove effective if the tree is in an active growing period, i.e. spring and summer.

UNDERGROUND SURPRISES

Gardeners generally tend to ignore what is not readily visible, and underground services are one of these aspects. Almost all domestic services enter the property under the ground, and if the current home owner is not there at the time of installation it is often simply assumed that they are 'out there somewhere'. Water, electricity, sewerage systems and in some cases gas and telephone facilities are all essential services for the running of any establishment, yet they are often ignored when creating a garden. Trees are planted within municipal servitudes, over water mains and sewerage lines, hard surfaces are installed over electrical, sewerage and water points and where telephone links are overhead, trees are often planted right under them.

Simple forward planning would avoid all the upheaval that is bound to occur in the future. The cost of tree removal is generally quite high, but not as costly as repairs to essential services that have been interrupted because plants or their roots have become entangled in them.

Plants are unaware of the source of moisture, only that it is available, and roots will tend to develop in its direction. Should that source be a poor sewerage connection or a weak water main joint, roots in the vicinity will develop towards this point. It is important to realise that any plant will have a root system underground as big, if not bigger than the visible part of the plant above the ground.

When planting large shrubs and trees

- Check with the local authorities to see if any servitudes exist on the property and where they are.

- Look for critical connections of any of the essential services such as water, sewerage and electricity as they enter or leave the property. Determine the depth of these services.

- Confirm the size of large shrubs and trees before purchase and decide where in the garden they can be planted without causing problems with the position of the services.

- Whether a tree has a taproot or a spreading root system, services in close proximity are at risk.

- If a problem with pipes and roots arises, expose the section of pipe, cut through the roots and after clearing away any roots from, or repairing, that section of pipe, encase it in reasonably strong concrete. This works where reasonable-sized shrubs and trees are involved.

- Large trees will need to be removed, or alternatively, redirect the service being affected.

Plant roots are aggressive: this is how plants are able to survive! Something as small and incidental as a pipe or cable will not get in the way of their development – so make sure they are kept well away from each other.

VEGETABLES

One of the most rewarding aspects of domestic gardening is growing vegetables. Being able to harvest something usable from the ground – something that went into the ground as a small seed or plant – is great motivation, but there is still the myth that vegetable gardening is an activity for the back garden, out of sight and away from the rest of the garden. This results in a section of the garden looking generally untidy, semi-neglected and far from attractive.

Vegetable gardening has recently come into its own again. This upswing in interest is due to several factors.

- New, interesting vegetable varieties are available from seed suppliers.
- A general awareness of healthier eating habits
- Gardeners are being made aware of the simplicity of vegetable gardening through the media and seed packet information.
- Vegetables are seen more as garden plants, and as a result are being used among other plants as foliage contrast while they are maturing.

Small garden spaces have helped to encourage this trend.

- Compact and colourful vegetables have become popular as potted plants or fillers in small spaces.

These and other individual reasons, such as cost, availability and an awareness of a more organic approach to gardening, have pushed vegetable gardening right into the spotlight.

When considering growing vegetables it is wise to have an area in mind, and to design and prepare it properly.

- Make sure it is in full sun.
- Provide a watering system, including a tap for washing off the finished product.
- Determine the extent of the area, provide serviceable pathways and some form of boundary demarcation.
- Don't make the beds wider than can be worked in without having to stand in them.
- If space is a problem, avoid trying to accommodate the large bulk crops such as onions, potatoes, maize and pumpkins, as they all take up a lot of space and in most cases it is easier to buy them than to find space to grow

sufficient in a domestic situation. (Farm gardens are an obvious exception.)

- Try to create beds with their length running north–south; this prevents the taller plants from casting too much shade on the smaller plants.
- Always try to rotate leaf crops with root crops, and don't plant the same type of crop in the same area twice without a break.
- Have some form of composting system nearby, as there is a generous amount of usable material when harvesting vegetables.

For the dedicated asparagus fan, they can easily be grown from seed as a garden ornamental and harvested too.

Rooting hormone – A chemical into which cuttings can be dipped, to induce and stimulate root development. Various 'strengths' are available for cuttings taken at different stages of the plant material's development.

Root cutting – A form of vegetative propagation that uses sections of some plants' roots to grow new plants. The mother plant is dug up and sections are cut off the root system; these are cut into pieces and replanted. Horseradish and *Acanthus mollis* can be grown in this way.

Runners – An alternative name for rhizomes, used when referring to the rhizomes of some grasses and bamboos.

Scarify – A process used to remove dead grass from a lawn area before the new growing season. This removal prevents a build-up of dead grass that could encourage fungal problems. Either a lawn mower, set low down, or a scarifying machine with rotating steel pins can be used for the purpose.

Seedling – Although this is the name generally given to young annuals, it applies to any newly germinated plant.

Soilless mixture – Growing medium formulated without the inclusion of soil. In most cases, the soil is replaced with either composted wood shavings or milled pine tree bark. These mixtures are generally lighter and increasingly

Some plants are constantly being improved on through hybridisation; the lowly indigenous 'Ivy-leafed' Pelargonium is one of these.

more popular for the indoor plant growing industry.

Stratification – A process that is used to assist in the germination of certain seeds, by softening the hard outer coating or simulating a winter period. Generally seed is sandwiched between layers of wet sand or moss, and kept cool for several weeks until germination begins, after which the seed is removed and planted out.

Species – Refers to groups of similar plants within a genus. For example, all the different rose species are called *Rosa* (genus), followed by specific species such as *banksiae*, *odorata* or *multiflora*.

Spring treatment – A process of levelling, feeding, scarifying and generally upgrading warm season (spreading) grasses such as kikuyu at the end of winter or in early spring before the surge of new growth.

Stolons – See 'runners'.

Thatch on grass – Another term for the build-up of dead grass on lawns.

Under-stock – The part of the plant that is used as a root system for any grafted or budded plants. Should any growth appear from this area it must be removed, as this is not growth of the required plant.

Vegetative propagation – Any means of reproducing plants that induces live material to root and grow, rather than using seed. Any of the conventional methods will produce plants that are identical to the mother plant.

Viable seed – Seed that is alive (has a live embryo) and has the ability to germinate.

Wood chips – A form of organic groundcovering or mulch made by passing freshly cut branches through a machine that carves the wood, leaves and bark into chips.

Woody perennial – Another name for a plant that does not die down in winter; more commonly referred to as shrubs and trees.

Mulch is anything organic or inorganic used to cover soil for various reasons. Here wood chips have been used.

WATER FEATURES

Much has been written on the pros and cons of installing and maintaining a water feature. The size of water features may vary considerably, but this is seldom as important as how well they are constructed, how effective the filtration and water movement systems are, and how efficiently they are maintained. A tiny portable water feature can prove to be more problematic than a large lake.

Efficient water feature maintenance is based on simple yet important aspects that begin at the time of construction.

■ If the pond is excavated, make sure that the final shape and edges are level.

■ Check that the general depth, channels and narrow parts of the water feature will be reasonably proportioned *after* the concrete shell has been cast.

■ If excavated areas are to be lined with plastic, make sure that plastic sheeting is available in widths suitable for the proposed water feature. The typical heavy-duty plastic sheeting used is only available in specific sizes and cannot

be permanently joined in any way that will make it watertight.

■ If prefabricated ponds are installed make sure they are level and deep enough to appear as a water-tight hole *in* the ground, not half *on* it!

■ Don't add rocks, boulders or pebbles at the time of casting the initial concrete shell, or throw the concrete around them, as this will cause the

shell to crack at the point where the stones and concrete meet, because they expand at different rates.

■ Where at all possible, include an outlet and drainage system, for emptying and cleaning, at the time of casting the initial concrete shell. Use galvanised water pipe and a suitable stopcock rather than PVC piping, as the concrete cannot adhere to the PVC.

Ponds add tranquillity to any garden setting but it's important to keep them well maintained. Remove the banned weed Pontederia cordata *(on the left), for example.*

Even small spaces can accommodate a water feature – here a hollowed out piece of sandstone overflows into a pebble-covered sump.

- When it is not possible to include a drainage point, slope the floor to a point where a pump can be used to remove the water.

- Add a waterproofing chemical to the plaster mix when finishing off the surface.

- Coat the entire shell with a suitable waterproofing compound; some techniques use a synthetic membrane as part of the process. If this is the case, use the membrane even if it is a messy task.

- Only when all of this has been completed can pebbles, boulders, rocks, etc. be added, with no fear of the structure leaking.

- If water is to be circulated from the pond to other structures and back again, make sure that all pipe connections and the various stages through which the water must flow are all entirely waterproof before adding any further detail, such as stones, structures and pumps or spray fittings.

- Electricity and water should never come in contact with one another, so it is extremely important that any electrical wiring is undertaken by a qualified electrician who is aware of what is intended and what power is required for lights and pumps. Make sure that any electrical fittings and their housings are weatherproof.

- Line the excavation with fine soft sand first if plastic is to be used as a pond liner, and do not walk in it once the plastic has been laid. Work from planks laid across the pond.

- Don't trim the plastic to shape until the pond has been filled with water and the plastic liner has been moulded to the excavated shape.

- If any water features are intended, such as statues, fountain fittings, rocks or any other quite heavy item, create a firm, level, reasonably sized platform for it to stand on, and build this as part of the excavated area *before* the plastic is inserted. Even top it with several layers of extra plastic once the liner is in place, making sure that there is no chance that the heavy item can pierce the plastic.

- Where possible, try to keep the exposed plastic edge to a minimum, as this is the area where perishing can occur, caused by UV exposure.

- After a plastic-lined pond has been filled to the maximum with water, pull the plastic tight and tidy up any folds. Add soil underneath the plastic in areas where it is not quite level. Place any surrounding such as brick paving, paving slabs or irregular rock at the same time as the excess plastic is cut off. In areas where waterside plants are to be grown, bury the plastic at least 20 cm deep, near the water's edge.

- At the same time, bury electrical cables and water piping in the same position or under any fixed surrounds to protect them during any further soil preparation.

- Koi fish have very specific requirements: if they are being considered for inclusion into the pond, consult a koi specialist before any form of construction takes place.

- A balanced pond – in terms of plant life, fish and clean water – is a healthy pond.

- A pond where the water is circulated is easier to keep healthy and clean.

- Don't construct ponds under the overhang, or in the dense shade of trees. Falling leaves can have an adverse impact on the quality of the water and the shady conditions tend to encourage the growth of algae.

- Clean out ponds at least every two to three years – replant the plants, scrub down the surface, service and clean pumps (do this a little more often perhaps), and refill with minimum delay. If the fish are kept in a smaller container during the process, keep them in a shaded position, *not* in full sun.

- Don't clean with any cleaning agents; scrub the surfaces with a stiff scrubbing or wire brush. Detergents could affect the fish when they are returned to the pond.

- If no fish are kept in the pond, it can be cleaned with a little swimming pool algaecide – or before pumping

An abstract figurine serves as a focal point to a simple pond in a geometric setting.

the water out, add granular chlorine to the water and allow it to stand for a day or two before emptying it out.

- Don't feed fish any more food than they can eat in a short time, as the residue can begin to affect the condition of the water.
- To keep birds from wading into ponds and catching the fish, run a single strand of wire around the edge of the pond roughly 30 cm above ground level and provide sheltered areas in the form of rocks or plants.

See AQUATIC PLANTS for further information.

WATER-WISE GARDENING
We live with the constant threat of drought. It would be foolish to consider gardening anywhere in South Africa without being aware of this fact. However, people will always want to grow something, and to make gardening possible without wasting water the principles of water-wise gardening were formulated early in the 1990s. Quite simply, they are a set of practical guidelines that allow the homeowner to enjoy gardening without unnecessary water wastage. Remember that water-wise principles are intended to conserve water, not to discourage gardening, although some of the suggestions will encourage gardeners to consider alternative options which are, as yet, not readily accepted.

- Reduce unnecessary lawn areas and replace these vast green areas with alternative groundcoverings such as gravel, bark chips or one of the many paving options.
- Consider using the more drought-resistant indigenous lawn options such as *Cynodon dactylon* hybrids rather than the more 'thirsty' lawns such as kikuyu.
- When designing new areas in the garden or replanting old revamped areas, try to group plants that have similar water requirements.
- Don't dig over the soil unnecessarily: this tends to dry out the soil and kill off beneficial enzymes and bacteria.
- Where possible, plant plants that need a lot of water in areas where evaporation is limited, under trees, in areas where there is less wind, in east- or south-facing positions or where soil is shaded by taller plants.
- Mulch any open, exposed soil areas to reduce evaporation; alternatively plant perennials or groundcovers that have low water requirements.

Select plants that all have the same water requirements for an effective water-wise garden.

- When selecting summer annuals, consider larger plantings of drought-resistant varieties such as petunia, marigold, *Zinnia*, *Alyssum*, sunflowers and *Vinca*, and limit the water-loving ones to areas of important focal impact or where other water-loving plants are being grown.

- Consider planting more plants in containers and use these containers in areas where colour is required.

- Consider glazed or painted containers as alternatives to unglazed and cement product ones: less moisture evaporates through the sides of the glazed or painted containers. Incorporate water-retaining chemicals in the soil mixes.

- Apply several coats of any waterproofing product to the inside of terracotta and other unglazed containers before painting, as this will help reduce evaporation.

- If a watering system is to be installed or an existing system is to be upgraded or extended, consider low-pressure micro-spray systems; alternatively, replace existing spray nozzles with low-angle spray nozzles – either way more water reaches the soil and evaporation is reduced.

- Any type of water timer can help to conserve water if programmed properly.

- There are irrigation systems that have been designed to reduce evaporation considerably. Some of these systems are installed under the soil, while others seep or drip into the soil at ground level.

- Regulate irrigation systems to spray during the early morning or late afternoon hours; this helps to keep evaporation to a minimum.

- In the summer rainfall areas, don't over-water the garden in winter when many plants are dormant or require less water. (This does not apply to winter-flowering plants.)

- A thorough watering, less often, is much better than regular light sprinklings, which encourage roots to develop near the surface where they can be dried out by the heat.

WEEDS AND WEEDING

Simply defined a weed is a plant that is undesirable in a specific area. Some plants have become weeds because they are prolific seeding plants, such as *Cosmos* or 'khakibos' others are weeds simply because they are growing in the 'wrong place' such as sunflowers growing in a rose garden or creepers growing up into neighbouring trees and shrubs. Irrespective of what constitutes a weed, the bottom line is that the sooner they are removed the better. Basically there are two methods of weeding.

Physical removal

Physically remove the weeds either by digging out the plants, or in a more satisfying way – by pulling them out manually. Ideally this must be done when the plants are young, before the plants flower and set seed – this makes weeding out further generations of the same weed much simpler. To make the task easier, wait until it has rained or weed after you have watered the area well and allowed the water to drain away a little. Once pulled out, do not leave the weeds to lie on the soil, rather have a plastic bag or bucket handy so that the weeds die and dry out in a contained space. If there are any seeds they won't fall back onto the soil.

Chemical control

The alternative method of weed control is chemical by nature – herbicides, some of which are in liquid form while others are granules, are applied at a prescribed rate per square metre. The most extreme method is to sterilise the soil with soil sterilant gases, containerised under pressure in canisters. This is a commercial process and not suitable for the homeowner because of the hazardous nature of the products. A more common alternative to this is to use herbicides to treat the soil surface or the specific plants.

The products available can be broad spectrum or non-selective, which means that they will kill or have an adverse impact on all or most plants they come in contact with, so it is important to apply the product only as directed so as not to kill the wrong plants. There are also selective or specific herbicides, some of which have been designed to kill specific plants growing among other plants. In this category there are herbicides that will kill specific grass types, broad-leafed weeds or select invader plants such as 'queen-of-the-night' cactus. There are herbicides that only kill plants if the product is sprayed on the green parts of the plants, whilst having no impact on the soil surrounding the plant. This product has great applications in the garden – from clearing weeds from paved areas to weed control of one plant among others, simply by dabbing the product on the specific plants.

Other herbicides have a long-term impact on the soil, such as those that are sometimes sprayed on open undeveloped land or pavements to control weed infestation. These must be used with extreme caution and only in extreme circumstances, where other weed eradication methods are not practical.

In more recent developments there are herbicides called pre-emergent herbicides, which prevent seed from germinating. Applied every six or so months, this is an ideal product to control weed germination in general flower beds once the soil has been prepared for the season, but remember that the product does not differentiate between weed and flower seed!

Points to remember

- In all cases where herbicides are to be applied it is important to use the correct safety attire and follow all mixing and application instructions to the letter.

- Remember to keep all herbicide spraying equipment well marked and away from spraying equipment used for other purposes.

- Don't apply spray herbicides if the wind is blowing. Make sure that the weather is clear and sunny with little chance of rain.

- Store all herbicide products out of the reach of children and casual staff in dry cool conditions.

- Don't spread any herbicides under newly laid paving. This will not prevent weed growth as most weed seed is windborne, but it may have an adverse effect on other plants nearby particularly if the site slopes and the water runoff can carry the product down to planted areas.

- Finally, it is better to cover garden spaces with plants or mulch to prevent weed germination and to use herbicides as an alternative rather than a constant method of weed control.

WILDLIFE

There are droves of birds, mammals, reptiles and (select) insects that any gardener would willingly invite into a garden. They are a part of the natural environment, which cannot be brought or created. Most wildlife will come and go as it pleases: other than trying to provide encouragement by creating an ideal habitat, the homeowner is generally quite helpless. It is important to remember that capture and caging of indigenous wildlife species are not allowed. This includes all those lovable creatures such as tortoises, monkeys, snakes, birds and bushbabies.

When trying to create the ideal environment or habitat for wildlife visitors, remember a few important points:

- Don't site nesting logs or feeder trays in areas where there is excessive traffic and movement, or in areas frequented by children and family pets. Feeding and nesting areas should rather be seen from a distance.

- Rather than provide artificial facilities such as feeder trays and birdbaths, try and mimic natural habitats by planting natural food plants and shelter, and creating areas where wildlife can feed, build nests or seek protection.

- If the area is known for a particular species, research its specific requirements before simply doing what 'looks' right. Speak to experts in the field and invest in well-written literature.

- Don't encourage wildlife to become dependent on the food you put out – you will not be doing the animals a favour!

- Should 'encouraged' wildlife become a problem (as can be the case with vervet monkeys and baboons), report it to the Department of Nature Conservation rather than trying to solve the problem personally.

- Thick, unattended undergrowth in parts of the garden less frequented than others often attracts rats and mice. Although there are traps, pellets and poison blocks available, it is simpler to invest in a family pet or two and actively work in all parts of the garden regularly. Similar areas, in quiet urban or rural environments, have been known to attract snakes, particularly if there are rodents to feed on. The family pet and general activity in all parts of the garden appear to act as a deterrent.

- Grazing and burrowing animals that tend to inhabit the more rural gardens can have a devastating effect on plants (and the state of the garden in general). Fences may help, but unless they are set quite deep into the soil they are not going to keep out rabbits, mongoose, porcupines or warthogs. The electrical pet control systems that are available, set 10 cm above the ground, have been suggested as a solution for the smaller animals; and more than one strand, the other set higher, could perhaps help control buck! Also see MOLES.

- Blood-soaked rags or creosote-impregnated rope hung among plants are said to help deter buck from eating everything in sight.

Birds can be great garden pest eaters, encourage them where possible.

A delightful visitor to any garden, the chameleon must be seen as an outdoor resident not *an indoor pet.*

Butterflies are such graceful gardeners and should be constantly encouraged into any garden for visible as well as functional purposes.

- To prevent birds repeatedly nesting in the roof and to discourage bees from returning to previous swarming locations either in the roof or any other inconvenient place, spray the area with diluted 'creosote' diluted 10:1 with cleaning solvent or turpentine. Oil of lavender is said to work too, but is expensive.

- Discourage weaver birds from stripping palms and similar plants for nesting material by planting a clump of sugar cane (in areas where it will grow) or sowing a small patch of *Eragrostis curvula*, an indigenous grass naturally used by the birds for nest building. Toy snakes hung in the trees are said to discourage their nest-building.

- Spray young palms and other plants that are pecked at by birds with a solution of alum mixed 1:1 with water; repeat the spray after watering or rainfall.

For further information refer to ENVIRONMENTAL CONTROL.

WOOD

Wood has always been a popular design and construction material in gardens. Even in ancient Greek, Roman and Egyptian gardens there were summer houses, benches, pergolas and plant supports made of wood – and one imagines that when these structures weathered and fell apart the homeowner simply made others. Today the cost factor causes gardeners to think ahead to preservation rather than elimination.

South Africa's climate can be harsh, with cold snaps, extreme heat, drought and constant damp, all in the space of a year. Repeat this pattern year after year, and untreated or poorly maintained wood will have an extremely limited lifespan.

Wood varieties are limited: the most readily available timber is pine, maranti or eucalyptus (saligna). The more exotic woods, such as teak, mahogany and keuring, are reserved for furniture, gates, designer summer-houses, patio coverings, and so on. Although local timber has had a poor track record as an outdoor product if uncared for, the products and expertise that are available today do extend its lifespan considerably.

- Consider which wood type will best be suited to the task at hand.

- Enquire if the wood is available as a 'Tanalised' timber (a process by which wood is impregnated with wood-preserving chemicals, under pressure, greatly extending its natural lifespan). 'Tanalised' wood has a natural pale green colouring, which can be disguised with any of several outdoor wood stains and colourants. It can also be left natural, and will age to a silvery-grey colour.

- Many wood-preserving materials are available, and care in selecting the right type of dressing is important. Some can be used together, one coated over the other; others cannot. Some penetrate into the wood (oil-based); others simply protect the surface (some varnishes).

- The product selected will determine the regularity with which the wood has to be treated, and how.

- If creosote is used to treat existing wood structures, the plants near or growing on the structure need to be protected against the fumes for a week or so, as they can seriously damage plant growth.

Hint: If wood is to be used as posts or upright supports, and embedded into concrete, make sure that the post extends a little below the concrete, rather than being entirely encased in it. This prevents the post ends from rotting off.

Well-kept outdoor wooden furniture will have a long functional life in all climatic conditions.

- For construction it is best to drill through the wood and use nuts and bolts for holding the structure together. The wood splits less and replacement is easier should the bolts rust. (Galvanised nuts and bolts are better and brass ones perfect, where appropriate.)

- Where possible, cap the tops of upright timber with metal caps to help preserve them against moisture damage. Similarly, wood uprights can be held in place by bolting them into metal fittings, which in turn can be inserted into concrete. (Several standard-sized fittings can be purchased from select hardware or timber outlets.)

- Timber walkways, stepping stones and wooden decks should not lie directly on the ground, as this results in the wood warping or rotting from moisture. It also encourages white ants (termites). Treat the underside of the wood with several coats of creosote and lay the treated timber on a 10 cm thick layer of sand. Alternatively, raise the wood slightly on bricks, concrete pillars or metal supports.

- When sculptural pieces of driftwood are used in the garden and cannot be treated (because of their visual artistic effect), raise the piece onto a low platform of bricks or paving slabs concealed by plant material or pebbles.

- Lattice panels or wood structures that are attached to walls should be mounted in such a manner that they can be removed for maintenance purposes – both of the wall and the panel. Hinge the bottom of the panel and hold it in place with a clasp, or hang decorative panels from two robust metal hooks.

- Wait for a dry period if wood is to be treated, to allow the item to dry out properly, and sand off any old weathered product or wood. Remove and replace any rotten or damaged parts of the structure.

- If the item is such that parts cannot be replaced, a sculpture or driftwood for example, chip away all the soft rotten wood until only firm healthy wood remains. Coat the surface with either a few coats of a systemic fungicide, a reliable tree sealer, or several coats of a weatherproofing product (with membrane). After this, the area may be built up with synthetic products until it becomes part of the original shape again.

- If tree stumps are kept after a tree has died, either as table bases, bird feeders or as climber supports, they will need to be treated to prevent them being eaten by white ants. Dust regularly with termite bait or, if no plants grow too near the base, paint around the base with several coats of creosote and allow it to weather for at least six months for the creosote to soak in before adding any plant material.

- Remember that all possible sides –

top, bottom, back and front – of any wood item that is exposed to weather conditions must be coated if the wood-preserving product is to be effective.

- If wood is used as mulch, in the form of wood chips, milled bark or bark nuggets, spread the material on woven plastic sheeting or a 7,5 cm thick bed of sand. This helps to keep the material clean. Some form of edging is advised to keep it in place too.

RIGHT: Wooden crafted sculptures need to be well treated if they are to have a permanent place in the landscape.
BELOW: Wooden railway sleepers are generally quite robust in harsh outdoor situations. Here they are being used to retain a bank.

XMAS (AND OTHER SPECIAL OCCASIONS IN THE GARDEN)

Special occasions like works parties, Christmas family gatherings, weddings, special birthdays, or any other out-of-the-ordinary event that is to be held in a garden are often a stressful occasion rather than a memorable one. Plants don't look as they should, and won't

Not simply to celebrate a festive season, holly, Ilex aquifolium, *is festive enough to plant anywhere and it loves the cold too.*

bloom; there are gaps in the flowerbeds and the grass has gone yellow or patchy; the garden help has gone on holiday and there's not time to solve the problems.

Any such event should be designed 'backwards': working from a day or so before the event, calculate how much time is needed to produce the effect desired. Should seed sowing be an option, check the time-span between sowing and flowering with the suppliers. If annuals are to be planted, which varieties must be planted first (because they take the longest time to reach flowering size), and which must be planted last. Instant colour is ideal for a 'quick-fix', but remember that most of the flowering material will be of a similar height and all quite low, roughly 30–40 cm only.

To add colour to dark, non-flowering areas of the garden, plant annuals or perennials in light-coloured containers and group them among the shrubs. When the event has a special colour scheme, as is often the case with weddings, Christmas and anniversaries, try to emphasise these colours in focal or important areas – this helps to unify the general appearance of the garden. Concentrate on areas of importance. If a tent is being erected; focus on the entrance and surrounds. Should the occasion be an evening event, concentrate all the plant detail (and subsequently the guests' attention), at the areas that will be illuminated.

If a specific area of the garden – the swimming pool or tennis court, for example – is all that will be in use, it is pointless to exert effort in any other parts of the property. Generally tidy them up and leave it at that. A neat and tidy garden often creates the best impression; after all, the guests are there for an event – and if that holds their attention, the garden is simply a backdrop to it all.

Its bright, simple red bracts make the Poinsettia a cheerful flower often linked with the spirit of Christmas. Generally it makes an ideal indoor flowering plant.

YEARLY GARDEN TASKS

Much to the relief of the gardener, some tasks are annual events rather than ongoing routine maintenance tasks. Such yearly projects often tend to be forgotten in the daily run of garden care, and although the tasks occur once a year, the timing is important: if overlooked, another year has to pass before the correct time comes again. A good idea is to diarise these tasks early in the new year (or use the Year Planner provided overleaf). This helps prevent mishaps and in some cases, plant and money losses. These once-off tasks can to some extent be divided into the four seasons or itemised month by month.

- Deciduous fruit trees such as peaches, nectarines and to a lesser extent apricots and plums must be pruned during winter – preferably before their buds swell or open.

- The later in the winter, and the colder the weather, the more of an ideal time it is to prune roses.

- *Hydrangeas* should be pruned by the time the fat buds at the base of the stems begin to swell and open.

- Spring bulbs should be in the ground by the end of April and at the very latest by mid-May in the Western Cape. Bulbs that are forgotten will not survive until the following planting time. Even if there is less chance that the late-planted bulbs will flower, plant them anyway.

- Sow Namaqualand daisy seed when the autumn weather is dry, but not too late (late April). Young plants that are still developing when the spring rains begin, suffer from rust and seed production is poor. Harvest their seed on a sunny, dry day and inspect daily so as to gather the maximum seed.

- Tall summer-flowering annuals should be planted by the end of October to be able to grow and flower before they are frosted.

- Summer bulbs can be frosted or begin to go dormant whilst still in prime flowering if planted too late.

- *Lilium* bulbs must be planted immediately they are purchased. They have no protective coating like true bulbs such as daffodils and onions to prevent them from drying out.

- Any wood repair work should be done in the warm dry period before the wet season and not after it. This way rot and other water-related problems are avoided.

- Plants that are kept for their dormant winter effect, ornamental grasses and some water plants must be cut back at the end of winter, before they begin to develop new growth for the spring season.

- Evergreen flowering perennials such as *Clivia*, hellebores, *Agapanthus*, *Irises* and *Hemerocallis* (day lilies) should be lifted and split as soon as possible after they have finished flowering, so that they re-establish themselves and develop the next flush of flowers without any undue stress.

- Deciduous plants, particularly roses and large trees, can only be moved with any level of success if moved in winter, the colder the better.

- Evergreen trees and shrubs move with difficulty: the best level of success is achieved if they are moved just before the emergence of the new season's growth.

- Seed lawns are best sown either in spring or autumn: summer is too hot or dry, and winter is either too dry or wet and cold, which will limit germination.

- Prune spring-flowering plants as soon as they have finished flowering so that they can develop new growth, with time enough for it to mature, ready to flower the following spring.

YELLOWING OF FOLIAGE

Some plants are almost better known for their yellow, sickly foliage than for their potential healthy appearance and flowers. Such can be the case with *Gardenia*, *Azalea*, some *Proteas* and *Ericas* and *Hydrangea* varieties. There is seldom too much cause for alarm, unless the plants have been affected by this condition for a considerable length of time and a fair amount of the foliage has already gone brown and fallen off.

Correctly speaking, this condition is known as 'chlorosis' and is common with acid-loving plants that have been planted in soil where the presence of too much lime (a very high pH, alkaline in other words) has prevented the plants from having access to essential iron minerals, resulting in the iron deficiency showing up as a yellowing of the foliage, stunted tip growth and little or no flowering. This problem is often caused in areas where building has recently taken place – a new development site, for example, where there is an excessive amount of cement in the soil. The problem can easily be corrected by dusting the area with 30 g of flowers of sulphur per square metre as a long-term solution and a foliar spray of iron chelate or trace element mixture applied as instructed on the container. This usually corrects the condition within a few weeks, but further one-monthly applications for a while longer will do no harm.

Despite the rather gloomy picture of yellowing plants appearing in odd parts of the garden because of a lack of iron, there are plants that have been cultivated for their golden variegated leaves. (Just as there are white or silver variegated forms of some plants.) The secret with growing these plants is to try and maintain the coloured form – the gold or silver appearance – and discourage any pure green parts of the plant, which may grow from time to time. Try to remove these parts of the plant entirely when they appear before they begin to dominate the plant, which they will do, quite vigorously. If the coloured foliaged plant has been grafted, as is the case with 'golden' forms of maple, elm and *Robinia*, the green growth may be produced below the graft and this growth will soon overwhelm the grafted form to the point that it may decline to the point of dying.

Other plants are generally gold and green all over, as is the case with 'golden' privet, *Ligustrum ovalifolium* 'Aureum' or *Abelia grandiflora* 'Francis Mason', the gold form of 'glossy' *Abelia*.

A general seasonal pruning in mid-summer will help to keep the plant tidy and assist in generating new 'gold' foliage.

Even more alarming than the simple gold forms of some plants is the trend to produce plants with a distinct lime green appearance. To the ill informed these have the distinct appearance of an underfed plant. They do need to be planted in sunny situations to retain their colour and even short periods of shade tend to reduce this colour to a rather sickly green. Sadly many of these lime green plants do suffer in the severe summer heat.

Lastly there are plants that annually turn yellow as the seasons move toward autumn. These plants are generally deciduous and the colouring of the leaves occurs as the old leaves begin to die at the end of their growing season. It's nothing to be alarmed about, even if it begins to happen before the autumn. This is often the case when the summer is hot and dry and the leaves die off prematurely.

Not all yellow leaves are sickly, some yellow as autumn approaches prior to their falling off the plants ...

... while other yellow foliaged plants are bred to add a foliage contrast to the garden.

JANUARY

Post holiday garden care is
now essential.

FEBRUARY

Sow winter seed for colour
and vegetables.

MARCH

A good time to sow 'shade-
over' and other seed lawns.

APRIL

Autumn warns us to
protect. So do so – use
hessian or grass.

MAY

Last chance to plant
Spring bulbs.

JUNE

A quiet time – use it to
plan new ideas for the
months ahead.

*J*ULY

Remember it's rose
pruning time – are your
secateurs sharp?

_____
_____
_____
_____
_____
_____
_____
_____
_____
_____
_____
_____
_____

*S*EPTEMBER

Spring could burst out all
over – make sure you feed
and water.

_____
_____
_____
_____
_____
_____
_____
_____
_____
_____
_____
_____
_____

*N*OVEMBER

It's a good time to 'dead-
head' and divide.
.

_____
_____
_____
_____
_____
_____
_____
_____
_____
_____
_____
_____
_____

*A*UGUST

Winds blow and the
ground dries – use mulch
and lots and now.

_____
_____
_____
_____
_____
_____
_____
_____
_____
_____
_____
_____
_____

*O*CTOBER

Feed if you want to see the
results of the nicest Month.

_____
_____
_____
_____
_____
_____
_____
_____
_____
_____
_____
_____
_____

*D*ECEMBER

Party time – but feed and
water your plants too!

_____
_____
_____
_____
_____
_____
_____
_____
_____
_____
_____
_____
_____

ZODIAC SIGNS AND THE GARDEN

Whether myth or reality, some gardeners believe that there is sense in considering astrology with regard to gardening. Like many esoteric approaches to life, the origins of the guidelines and methods employed when gardening in conjunction with the zodiac signs have been lost in centuries past. However, that they are still practised today implies that in one way or another they offer an element of success. Just how involved the zodiac was with gardening in the past is not all that clear, but information regarding what gardening practices relate best to the various signs (and times of the year) does exist.

The zodiac signs are evenly distributed between four element groups:

- Water signs – Cancer, Scorpio and Pisces are root days, and when the moon passes in front of these signs it is seen as the ideal time to transplant almost anything.
- Earth signs – Taurus, Virgo and Capricorn are known as leaf days, and when the moon passes in front of these signs it is an ideal time to plant leaf vegetable crops.

- Fire signs – Leo, Aries and Sagittarius are regarded as fruit days, and when the moon passes in front of these signs, it is an ideal opportunity to plant fruit trees.
- Air signs – Aquarius, Libra and Gemini are regarded as flower days, and when the moon passes in front of these signs it is a great time to plant flowering plants – but rather weed and rest during Gemini!

With each of these signs certain gardening practices are favoured.

- Air and fire signs are for contemplation and meditation, both in and about the garden.
- On air days, stake climbers and sow seed of flowering plants.
- Sow flowering climbers in Gemini and annuals in Libra and Aquarius (autumn and spring)!
- Fire days are for healing and blessing the garden.
- For good health, sow plants in Aries.
- Plants sown in Sagittarius will grow vigorously and become tall.
- Leo is too cold to garden, and is a time to plan and design.
- The water signs are for wet work: water well and plant at this time.

- Never harvest fruit and vegetables during Pisces, as they will have a short shelf life and rot quickly.
- Vegetables should be harvested during Aries, and fruit in Taurus.
- For sweet leaves (herbs) and juicy fruit sow on water signs.

For Virgo there is the lily …

- Don't preserve crops that are sown or harvested during Aries.
- Earth signs are for working in and with the soil, digging, sowing, thinning out and transplanting.
- Weed extensively during Virgo.
- Capricorn is an excellent feeding time (so, incidentally, is Scorpio).
- Virgo is an ideal time to spray against pests with herbal sprays.
- Gather seed during Taurus and Capricorn.
- Vegetables and fruit that are hot to the taste, e.g. chillies and mustard, are best harvested during Scorpio and Leo.

Certain plants relate directly to specific Zodiac signs and are said to perform better during their sign month.

Aquarius – Southernwood (*Artemisia* species), marigold, foxglove, walnut and pine. Southernwood is an excellent insect repellent.

Pisces – Chamomile, mint, heliotrope, carnation, poppy, *Verbena* and violet. Use mint teas for relaxation and insect repellents.

Aries – Garlic, nasturtium, thistle, wild roses, stinging nettle, holly and edible chestnut. Stinging nettle makes an excellent blood-purifying tea.

Taurus – Tansy, sage, cherry, ash, myrtle, thyme, almond and apple. Both thyme and sage are excellent culinary herbs – but don't add too much sage, as it has a strong flavour, which will overwhelm all other herbs used.

Gemini – Caraway, dill, snapdragon, fern, *Iris*, parsley and elderberry. Caraway is ideal for pickling, and both caraway and dill for cooking fish. Parsley is an excellent breath freshener, especially after eating garlic.

Cancer – Chickweed, water lily, willow, privet, honeysuckle, lettuce and watercress. Although chickweed is regarded as a weed, it is an excellent fresh salad component.

Leo – *Calendula*, sunflower, laurel, *Forsythia*, palm and oak. *Calendula* (pot marigold) petals are tasty in salads and omelettes.

Virgo – Fennel, rosemary, Madonna lily and cornflower. Eat fennel to still hunger pangs; ideal to use with baked fish.

Libra – Pennyroyal, feverfew, violets, plum, *Nigella* (love-in-the-mist), and white roses. Pennyroyal is an ideal groundcover near patios or any other outdoor recreation areas, as it repels mosquitoes.

Scorpio – Horseradish, blackberry, basil, *Chrysanthemum* and purple *Erica*. Apart from using the pickled roots of horseradish, the new foliage is an interesting and refreshing addition to spring salads.

Sagittarius – Carnation, wallflower, mulberry, vine, dandelion, clover and pinks (bedding *Dianthus*). Dandelion is excellent as a tonic for jaundice and liver overload as well as being an excellent salad component.

Capricorn – Comfrey, rue, snowdrops, and cypress. Comfrey is an excellent compost activator and helps heal bones, bruises and cuts.

Interesting how many of the zodiac signs, their plants and their particular applications coincide with and apply to the southern hemisphere's seasons and seasonal activities!

Pisces and Sagittarius have carnations, and ...

Aquarius has the foxglove.

EPILOGUE

I probably could have written a book ten times thicker than this, had it fitted with wheels to cart it around by, and still not have been able to include all that could be said about maintaining a garden, with all of its aspects, many of which are unique to every individual garden. I trust that as you have wandered through the topics, pictures and pages you have been able to find the facts and solutions you need.

REFERENCES

Elwell, Henry & Maas, Anita. 1995. *Natural Pest and Disease Control.* Natural Farming Network Zimbabwe.

Henderson, Lesley. 2001. *Alien weeds and invasive plants.* Plant Protection Research Institute Handbook No. 12.

Malherbe, I. de V. 1964. *Soil Fertility.* Cape Town: Oxford University Press.

Sheat, W.G. 1982. *The A to Z of Gardening in South Africa.* Cape Town: Struik.

Van Wyk, Ben-Erik & Gericke, Nigel. 2000. *People's Plants.* Pretoria: Briza.

Von Breitenbach, J. et al. 2001. *Pocket List of Southern African Indigenous Trees.* Pretoria: Briza.

PHOTO CREDITS

Key: l = left, r = right, t = top, b = bottom, c = centre, D = detail. Grouped Detail photos are identified clockwise from top left corner as follows: D1, D2, D3, D4.

All photography by **Lynton V. Johnson**, except for the following:

Connell Oosterbroek: Front cover – inset pictures lcr; Title pages – top row 1, 2, 4, middle row 1, 2, 3, bottom row 4; Dedication page; Contents pages; p.viii; p.ix; p.1 D2, D4; p.2 bl, D; p.3 tc, br; p.4; p.5; p.8 Dl; p.14 D1, D2, D3; p.15 D; p.16; p.18; p.19; p.20; p.21 D1, D3, Dl, br; p.22 D3; p.24 Dl; p.25 D2; p.26 D; p.27; p.30; p.31 br; p.32; p.33 D1, D2; p.36 br; p.37 D3; p.39 D, b; p.43; p.45 D2, D3, Dl; tl, tr, bl, br; p.47 t; p.48 Dr; p.50 D3, b; p.51; p.52; p.53 Dl, Dr; p.54 D; p.55 D1, Dl, Dr; p.56 Dl, Dr; p.57 D; p.59 D1, Dl; p.60 D; p.62 Dl; p.64 D4; p.68; p.69 Dtr; p.70 Dl, Dr; p.71 l; p.72 D4, Dl; p.73 D1, D4, Dl; p.74 D; p.75 t, b; p.76; p.84 D; p.85 tr; p.86 D1, D2, Dr; p.87 b; p.91 D1, Dl; p.92 D2, D3, D4, Dl; p.93; p.95; p.96; p.97 b; p.98 D3, D4; p.104 tr; p.106 D3; p.110 D2, Dl; p.111.

Ball Straathof: Title pages – bottom row 3; p.2 br; p.6 tl; p.15 l; p.37 D4; p.42; p.59 b; p.92 D1, br; p.94.

South African Garden and Home: Front cover – main photograph; p.x; p.37 D1, D2; p.38; p.39 tl; p.40–41; p.73 D2, D3; p.74 b; p.80 D; p.81; p.86 D4; p.90; p.97 t; p.98 D2; p.95 tl; p.106 Dl; p.112; p.113.

Hadeco: Title pages – bottom row 1, 2; p.8 D2, D4; p.11; p.12; p.13 t; p.59 D4; p.105 d4; p.110 D1, br.

Pitta Joffe: p.1 D1; p.7; p.22 Dl, b; p.47 D; p.69 Dl; p.97 Dl; p.98 tl, tr.

Ben-Erik van Wyk: p.25 D3, D4; p.28; p.31 bl; p.64 D1, D3; p.69 Dbr; p.70 tl, ct, cb; p.72 D3; p.78 D1, Dl, br; p.105 D3, bl.

Frits van Oudtshoorn: Title pages – top row 3; p.48 Dl, bl; p.59 D2; p.63 b; p.65 br; p.67 t.

Gardena: p.49; p.71 br; p.84 tr, p.86 Dl.

Fanie Venter: p.79.

INDEX